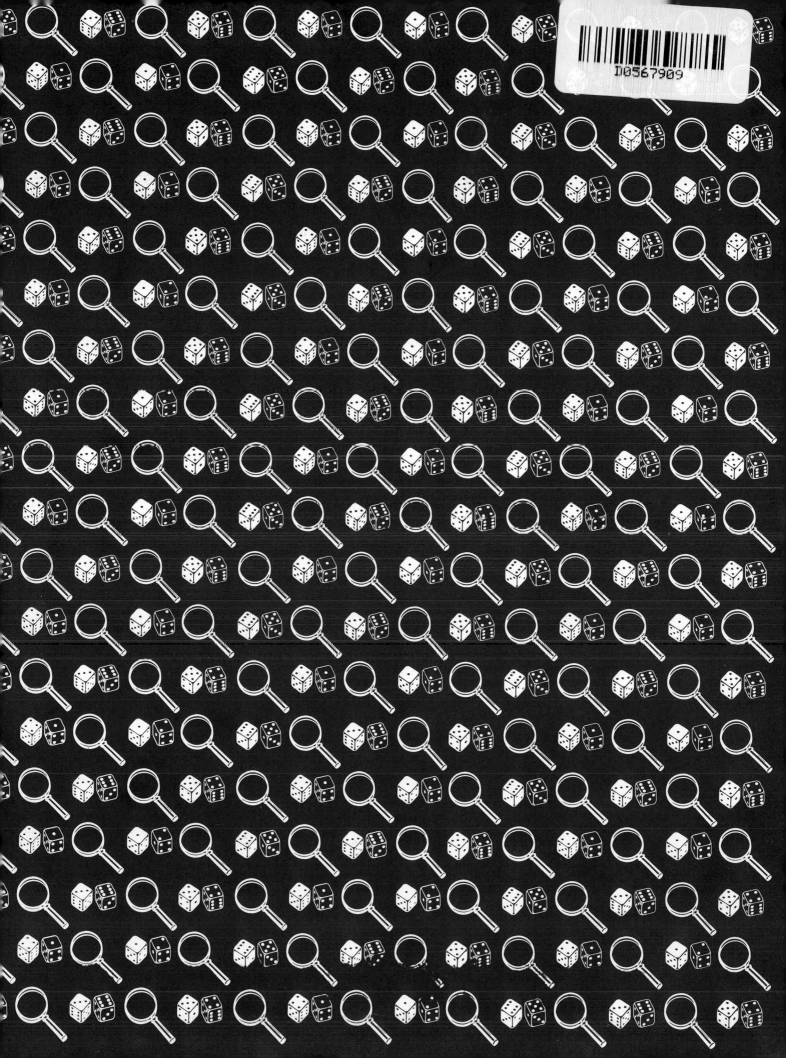

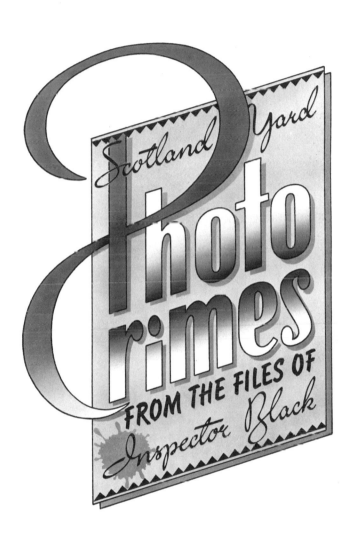

Scotland Yard

Photo Crimes

FROM THE FILES OF

Inspector Black

Producer
Amy Carroll
Director
Denise Brown

Continuity
Debra Grayson
Wardrobe & Props
Melanie Miller

First published in Great Britain in 1983 by
Dorling Kindersley Limited, 9 Henrietta Street,
Covent Garden, London WC2E 8PS

Manufactured in Singapore

10 9 8 7 6 5 4 3 2 1

Library of Congress Cataloging in Publication Data
Main entry under title:

Photo crimes from the files of Inspector Black of
Scotland Yard.

1. Puzzles. 2. Detective and mystery stories.
GV1507.D4P48 1983   793.73   83-11084
ISBN 0-671-47303-4

Scotland Yard
Photo Crimes
FROM THE FILES OF
Inspector Black

VOLUME I

SIMON AND SCHUSTER · NEW YORK

Dear Reader,

Inspector Henry Black (1890–1963) was one of Scotland Yard's finest detectives, and my great-uncle. He was among those few who were responsible for refining the techniques of criminal investigation and, in part, creating the modern detective. Evidence was all that mattered to him. He believed that only education and experience could make a good detective, and that familiarity with both typical and atypical physical evidence was a necessity.

Great-uncle Henry was a passionate communicator and copious note-taker. He was always ready to pass on his expertise in crime solving to his contemporaries and even to myself, his much-admiring great-niece. Long before he retired from the force, but after he was taken off active duty, he used to instruct younger colleagues on the finer points of detection with reference to his "master" cases. These consisted of a range of incidents — murders, kidnappings, thefts, suicides, extortions — which had occurred during the height of his investigatory career in the 1930s. Each case was a testimony to his genius as a crime solver.

He used to present these cases in the form of a slide show accompanied by notes of how he had proceeded. His students were then required to identify the culprits and give their explanations of how the deeds were accomplished. If the class had trouble reaching the correct solution, they could refer to certain clues and the suspects' statements. Great-uncle Henry's cases were extremely popular, but time changes most things and when he retired, so did his file. It was packed away in the attic along with his other memorabilia after his death.

And there it might have stayed were it not for a chance conversation at a crime writer's convention. A member of the association, and a chief inspector at Scotland Yard, was bemoaning the lack of detecting talent among new recruits. "No one seems to know a good clue from a red herring anymore. Crime laboratories are fine", he went on, "but these chaps think it's all done there."

That set me thinking. Perhaps Great-uncle Henry's master cases needed to be recalled from oblivion. He'd made crime solving fun while at the same time instilling a healthy respect for evidence. Perhaps, I thought, it was now up to me to see that his detecting acumen reached a wider audience.

Photo Crimes, then, is my attempt to make Great-uncle Henry's file a test of detecting ability for today's reader. I've left the cases as he wrote them up, including some of his master observations, all relevant clues (and some red herrings just as he would have used), the suspects, and his descriptions of what actually did happen, but I've presented his slides as photographs. Great-uncle Henry's marking system also can be used to keep score and preserve the "game" quality of his cases. You win or lose points according to the time elapsed, number of clues referred to, whether you chose the right or wrong suspect, or the right suspect for the wrong reason, etc.

You'll find that Great-uncle Henry's cases will require concentration, keen powers of observation, and a good understanding of character as well as the ability to think things through.

As you go through the book, keep a record of your score for each case on your Master Record, see page 64. At the end you'll discover whether Great-uncle Henry would have thought you Scotland Yard material or not.

Good luck and good detecting!

4

HOW TO PLAY THE GAME

Have handy a pencil or pen and a piece of paper to make notes, your scorecard to record your points and penalties, and a clock or watch to record your time. Then:

1. Read each case through carefully, studying the pictures and captions;

2. If you haven't a clue as to how it was done or by whom, turn to one or more of the clues listed, but remember — they cost you points;

3. If you think you know who the culprit is, answer the questions on his or her suspect's "card". *Bear in mind that in "suicide" cases, the victim can also be questioned.*

4. Look up your answer on the evidence pages. If you've proved your detecting ability you will be awarded points and a chance to look at the truth; if your crime solving is not up to the mark, you will lose points and may be advised either to look at a clue or try another suspect;

5. When you've answered correctly and have read the truth, make sure you have entered the correct points and penalties on your scorecard. Then add your overall score to your Master Record under the appropriate case heading.

Had she shot herself elsewhere and been moved to the bed?

Yes **1**   No **2**

Could she have had a disagreement with her husband?

Yes **3**   No **4**

Ans. **J** ....

CLARISSA DAVENPORT

You must answer both questions, in which case your final answer will always consist of a letter and a number. In this example, if you think the answer to both questions is "Yes", you would write 13 on the answer line. When you refer to the evidence your answer will be under 13, line J.

HOW TO SCORE

Different points and penalties are awarded depending on the difficulty of the case, the time if takes you to reach the correct solution, the number of clues referred to, and how many suspects you have to question.

The Cases
Great-uncle Henry classified his cases as easy, medium and difficult. You will be awarded 100 points for the correct solution to an easy case; 150 points for a medium one and 200 for a difficult case. When you've chosen the right suspect and answered the questions correctly, you will find your winning score on the evidence page.
NB As a police cadet you are considered to have accumulated 50 points before you begin on your first case, Final Curtain. Make certain you add this to your score, but only once.

Time
Easy cases earn 20 points if done within 15–20 minutes, 10 points if done in 20–30 minutes but no bonus points if it takes you more than 30 minutes; medium cases earn 30 bonus points if done in 15–20 minutes, 20 points if done in 20–30 minutes and 10 points if over 30 minutes; difficult cases earn 40 bonus points if done in 15–20 minutes, 30 points if done in 20–30 minutes and 20 points if it takes you over 30 minutes.

Clues
Each clue costs you 10 points in a difficult case, 15 in a medium one and 20 in an easy case. Red herrings are the same in all, minus 20 points from your score.

Suspects
The questions accompanying the suspects are supposed to test your detecting ability. Therefore, all completely wrong answers cost you 30 points, but if you answer the questions correctly, even though the suspect is wrong or, if you chose the right suspect but answer the questions incorrectly, you will lose between 10 and 25 points.

EASY	MEDIUM	DIFFICULT
Final Curtain	Industrial Espionage	Locked Room Mystery
Concerning Colnaghi	Going for Broke	Robbery on the
A Rendezvous with Death	The Basil Street Incident	Paddington Express
Death of a Lodger	An End to Life	Diamonds Aren't Forever
Bridal Grief	Accidents Do Happen	Black on the Beat
Dead Man's Tale	Theft at a Seance	The Park Lane Affair
	The Kidnapped Baby	
	Motive for Murder	
	The Purloined Pounds	

Accidents Do Happen

SUSPECTS					TOTAL
−25 150					125
CLUES					
−15 −15					−30
TIME					

minutes	15–20	20–30	30+
Easy	20	10	0
Medium	30	20	10
Difficult	40	30	20

TIME: 30

FINAL SCORE **125**

In the above example, the player has questioned one wrong suspect (losing 25 points) before guessing the culprit (earning 150 points). He or she has referred to two clues (losing 30 points) and completed the puzzle in good time (earning 30 points). The player would thus have won 125 points for that puzzle.

WHO CAN PLAY?

Photo Crimes can be worked singly, with a partner or against a competitor or competitors. For scoring, you can duplicate the score cards simply by tracing over the one in the book.

THE PIMLICO PLAYERS PRESENT

A·N·T·H·O·N·Y
AND
C·LE·O·PA·T·R·A

Proprietor : A. MARKS

Matinees : Tues & Sat 2·30
Evenings : 8·00

FINAL CURTAIN

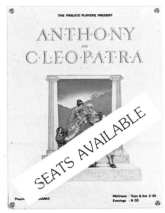

One of several necessary conditions for the obtaining of a confession is to have incriminating evidence against the suspect, which he understands to be so.

1 The Pimlico Players were reputed for their highly artistic productions, but their efforts were less than profitable. The only one who reaped any benefit at all was Alec Marks, the company's crafty producer and man-about-town.

2 He took pride in putting on a good show — for his friends. His paramours wore the latest Paris gowns, dined in the best restaurants, and drank the finest champagne.

3 In odd moments between rehearsals, the actors grumbled about their dwindling finances and Marks' new suits.

4,5 One afternoon Marks examined the books. The outlook was dismal. He could just manage his holidays, but there would be little left for the actors' salaries.

6 That evening's rehearsal went well, despite the actors' discontent. They'd played to a small audience last week, and worried about the troupe's future.

7 After the rehearsal, Marks broke the news to his leading actors — Godfrey Miller, Wallace Goodhew and Grace Peattie. He told them he was forced to close the show — they'd be out of work indefinitely.

8 Miller took out his long-suffering landlord's ultimatum: he had two days in which to pay his back rent. "I'll fix him!" he muttered.

9 Miss Peattie ran to her dressing-room, sobbing wildly. How would she be able to look after her invalid mother? "He can't do this to me!"

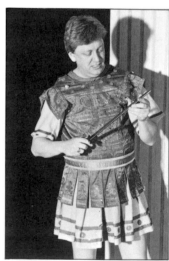

10 Goodhew cursed the producer as he felt the sharp edge of his sword. "I'll make that cad think twice about not paying!" he said.

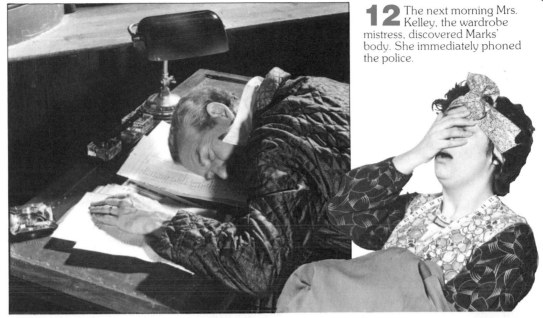

11 Once the three had gone and he was alone in the building, Marks went back over the books, hoping to juggle what was left of the funds to his advantage. He never heard the fatal footsteps behind him, but just before he died he caught a glimpse of his assailant.

12 The next morning Mrs. Kelley, the wardrobe mistress, discovered Marks' body. She immediately phoned the police.

The Inspector calls

13 Among the items on the desk were bank statements, a small round piece of metal and the murder weapon. **Under the victim's hand a "G" was written in blood.**

14 The Inspector questioned the only three members of the troupe whose names started with "G". Holding the murder weapon, he noted their immediate reactions.

GODFREY

15 Miller appeared to be angry and insulted. "I may have hated the dirty scoundrel," he said, "but murder is not in my repertoire."

WALLACE

16 Goodhew made a menacing gesture, then checked himself. "You can ring my wife," he sneered, "I was home all night. I didn't kill him."

GRACE

17 Miss Peattie gazed appealingly at Inspector Black and pouted. "Well, you certainly don't think *I* hit him, do you, Inspector?"

????????????????????????????

Inspector Black studied the faces of the three suspects glumly. He doubted that the lab report would be able to reveal the guilty party. Luckily, however, he knew who it was. Do you?

Chance a clue? **20, 30, 49**

Choose your suspect:
Wallace Goodhew, p.53
Godfrey Miller, p.54
Grace Peattie, p.54

CONCERNING COLNAGHI

The correct interpretation of evidence is necessary not only to identify the actual wrong-doer but just as vitally, to protect any innocent participants.

1 Mrs. Carruthers knew an authentic masterpiece when she saw one, and she was glad that the dealer she had visited that morning did not.

2 It was the find of her life — an original Colnaghi. She hung it proudly in her entrance hall. "It's almost immoral!" she laughed to herself. "Five pounds for a painting worth hundreds!" She could hardly wait to show off her find to her guests, who would be arriving any minute.

3 The first was her brother, Tim Waverly. He admired her extensive art collection, but he didn't know much about art. His hobby was spending his trust fund.

4 Robin Steinmetz, an art dealer and old friend, came next. Then John Hodgson arrived. He was head of a shipping firm, but he loved art and spent more time at auctions than he did at the office.

5 They all sat and talked about the masterpiece over cocktails. "Amazing," Steinmetz declared, "It's genuine all right — and for five quid! You wouldn't consider working for me, would you Dorothy?" They both laughed.

6 "How does she do it?" Hodgson whispered to Waverly. "I've spent years walking round shops, but I've never come across a find like that."

7 By 10 p.m., the guests had left. Mrs. Carruthers went upstairs to bed. She tossed and turned for hours, then went down for another look at her painting. **It was gone!**

8 In the morning, Inspector Black sent round his junior, P.C. Hobbs. He surmised that the thief had got in through the window — the hall was on the ground floor. He could find no fingerprints or footprints. The sitting room appeared to be undisturbed. Then Hobbs noticed that the bureau in the sitting room had been ransacked.

9 He found a pair of cuff-links and five one-pound notes in the drawer. It was clear that the culprit was only after the painting.

10 Hobbs checked the hall. There was a deep scratch near the bottom of the chair. Mrs. Carruthers was certain that it hadn't been there before. On another small table was a scarf and a pair of gloves. "My brother always forgets something," the woman explained, "I expect he'll be back this afternoon to claim them."

?????????????????????????????
Hobbs reported back to Inspector Black, for he hadn't a clue as to the identity of the culprit. Can you help?

Chance a clue? **10, 40**

Choose your suspect:
John Hodgson, p.53
Robin Steinmetz, p.56
Tim Waverly, p.56

A RENDEZVOUS with DEATH

Strangulation is one of the most commonly encountered methods of killing. When carried out with bare hands it is an unmistakably deliberate form of murder and can never be confused with an accident or suicide.

1 One breezy mid-March morning George Halliday made his way along a track in Littlewick Wood and stopped near a large old tree. He took a letter from his pocket and reread it. "I'll give this fellow a big surprise," he thought. He looked around nervously, but could see no one.

2 Five minutes later another man came down the same path, halted abruptly, and dodged behind some bushes. He peeked out carefully. Had he been seen?

A few minutes later Halliday was dead!

3 A forest keeper, making his usual morning rounds, had heard a muffled scream. He searched all round, came out into a clearing, and ran right into tragedy. A man was stretched out on the ground. No one else was in sight. The keeper ran to the main road and sent a car to the police station. Soon Inspector Black arrived.

4 The Inspector knew most of the residents in the district and he recognised Halliday at once. He had been brutally strangled. Inspector Black examined the stick which was lying near the body.

5 Then the detective turned his attention to the scene of the crime, making a close examination of the ground underneath the tree where the dead man lay. He noticed an envelope, addressed to Mrs. Halliday, the dead man's wife.

6 Next he picked up the hat which was a few feet away from the body and checked it carefully. He found a hair inside, which, when held up to the light, proved to be very black and curly.

A letter which spoke volumes

7 In the dead man's pocket was a letter to Mrs. Halliday. This young woman was often the subject of gossip, as she was something of a flirt. Currently, there were two men of the town who were known to be involved with her, and one had sent this letter.

Mrs Daphne
The

My darling girl,

I cannot let a week of eternity pass before I can feel your lovely arms around my neck and bury my face in your glorious hair.

I beg you to meet me under the Old Tree on Tuesday at 11:30. Be careful what you tell George, as I thought he looked suspicious the other day — but come, my dearest!

I count the hours until you can be with me again.

Oceans of Love
P.

8 When the Inspector called in on Phillip Sykes, a gentleman farmer who was often seen riding with Mrs. Halliday, the young man was cleaning his boots. "You must have been out in some pretty muck," the Inspector observed. Then he told Sykes all about the body found in Littlewick Wood.

9 "You've no reason to haul me off to gaol," Sykes said defensively. "A man's free to have a walk if he wants."

10 The Inspector then visited Mrs. Halliday's other "friend", a solicitor named Percy Carrington. He noted the hat and gloves on the table, as well as the stick, which had fresh mud on it. Carrington said he had just returned from seeing a client.

?????????????????????????????

Fate was unkind to George Halliday. Which one of his rivals killed him, and what's your evidence?

Chance a clue? **19, 29, 57, 60, 63, 65**

Choose your suspect:
Percy Carrington, p.52
Phillip Sykes, p.56

DEATH of a LODGER

An experienced practical investigator is not likely to overlook obvious clue materials which may include blood, spent bullets or cartridges, paint chips, fingerprints and the like. But even such a one must be alert when faced with evidence in other forms.

1 Late one night Inspector Black was summoned to a lodging house in one of the less desirable neighbourhoods of Camden Town. After waiting several minutes at the door, he was met by the landlord, a Mr. Samuel Quigley.

2 As they climbed the stairs, Inspector Black found Quigley to be a man of few words — only nods and grunts.

3 When they reached the second floor, Quigley pointed out the room in which a gruesome scene awaited.

4 The body of an elderly man lay on the floor, the face was contorted as though he had died from poison. "Simmonds," Quigley said when the Inspector asked the lodger's name. "When did you find the body?" the Inspector queried. "'Bout an hour and a half ago," said Quigley. "I was calling to collect the rent, and he didn't answer, though I knew he was in because I saw him come in earlier."

5 Simmonds' right hand lay open. Next to it was an old photograph of an attractive young woman, perhaps a former sweetheart. The Inspector examined it.

6 In Simmonds' left hand was an ordinary white linen handkerchief. The Inspector carefully drew it from the clenched hand, which was very cold.

7 Then he took a closer look at the handkerchief. It was new or freshly laundered. The name "Peck" was embroidered in one corner. Inspector Black put the handkerchief in his pocket for safe-keeping.

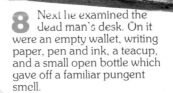

8 Next he examined the dead man's desk. On it were an empty wallet, writing paper, pen and ink, a teacup, and a small open bottle which gave off a familiar pungent smell.

9 Inspector Black read the pitiful suicide letter that had been lying on the desk. Quigley said that he recognised the writing as Simmonds'. The Inspector asked more questions but all he learned was that Simmonds had been a mysterious man who had kept to himself.

10 Then he picked up the teacup and studied it carefully. One sniff was enough to confirm his impression. **The "tea" was laced with poison.**

12 The other lodger, Ted Peck, was called in. The Inspector showed him Simmonds' body. "I don't know anything!" Peck protested vigorously, "I've been out looking for work all day and I was so exhausted, I turned in early."

11 The Inspector asked the sour-faced landlord if Simmonds had had any friends. "Can't really say," Quigley replied. Then Inspector Black asked whether the name "Peck" meant anything to him. "That'll be 2C," Quigley said.

???

Had Simmonds taken his own life, or was it taken from him?

Chance a clue? **9, 39, 48**

Choose your suspect:
Ted Peck, p.55
Samuel Quigley, p.55
Harold Simmonds, p.56

15

BRIDAL GRIEF

All good detective work is based on the recognition of significant details and the proper evaluation of their meanings. If an inference is to be correct it must be borne out by a number of circumstances.

"M-my wife has shot herself!"

1 stammered a distraught Mr. Davenport to the police. "I think she's dead. . . ."

2 Inspector Black was soon there. He was impressed at the opulence around him, but not surprised; everyone knew that the new Mrs. Davenport was worth millions.

3 Davenport led Inspector Black upstairs. When they approached the door to the master bedroom, he puffed nervously on his cigarette. The Inspector could see a young woman lying across the bed.

The husband's sad story

4 "Today was our first anniversary," Davenport began after composing himself. "We had reservations for dinner at The Paradise Lounge — our favourite restaurant. Clarissa seemed in a good mood. She even asked me to select which of her gowns she should wear. Once dressed she looked a vision! I told her she'd never looked more beautiful. Then I went downstairs for a drink while she applied her finishing touches.

5 I sat downstairs for about ten minutes, relaxing over my gin and tonic. Suddenly I heard a loud bang! I jumped to my feet and ran upstairs. When I rushed into the room, there she was, lying across the bed. I got to the phone as quickly as I could."

6 Inspector Black examined the body. The bullet had entered the temple and passed through her skull. The gun was still in Mrs. Davenport's hand.

7 No, Davenport couldn't think why his wife would have killed herself. "She was very upset about a letter she received yesterday, but she wouldn't show it to me."

8 The Inspector then asked if he might use the telephone. He went downstairs and phoned The Paradise Lounge. Yes, they did have a reservation in the name of Davenport. It was for a table for two at 9 o'clock.

9 When Inspector Black returned, he continued his investigation. The Davenports' room was full of objets d'art, but nothing seemed out of place. He did, however, find two hairpins on the carpet.

10 Then he examined the dressing table. There were the usual items: lipstick, powder, rouge and perfumes.

11 In the drawer he found a number of unpaid bills for men's clothing from the best Saville Row shops, but no letter.

??
As far as Inspector Black could tell, Davenport's story was credible. Or was it? Was this suicide — or murder?

Chance a clue? **18, 28, 59**

Choose your suspect:
Clarissa Davenport, p.52
Gerald Davenport, p.53

DEAD MAN'S TALE

It is well known to crime investigators that in cases of suicide the method of its commission is often dictated by fashion. If there are certain variations in the procedure they are likely to give rise to suspicions of foul play.

1 Inspector Black rushed to the home of Mr. and Mrs. Hamilton. Mr. Hamilton had been found hanging in the attic. The Inspector went up and saw the body lying on the floor. There was a severe bruise on the right temple, and a deep mark around his neck from the rope. He had been dead at least an hour.

2 The Inspector noted that the rope tied round Hamilton's neck matched exactly the end that was still hanging from a hook in the skylight.

3 Then he took a careful look at the body. The smart suit Hamilton was wearing looked rather new, but it was quite dusty on the back.

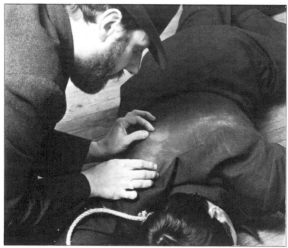

4 His shoes were of first-class quality; Hamilton had been a man with expensive tastes. Having made a quick but thorough examination of the body, Inspector Black turned his attention to the room.

6 The rest of the attic was bare, except for an old waste-paper basket, a broom, and a battered suitcase.

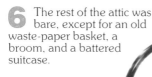

5 The floor was dusty, particularly near the door, where dirt had been swept by someone using the room.

7 The Inspector went downstairs to talk to Mrs. Hamilton. She was distressed, and admitted that her husband had been very angry earlier that day.

8 "It all started when Giles came home for lunch," Mrs. Hamilton began. "He and his brother had words. Laurence has been living with us for a few months now."

A possible motive?

9 Giles had accused Laurence of paying too much attention to her, and told him to leave. "'I was a happy man before you came,' Giles had said. Laurie rushed out. I wanted Giles to calm himself, so I went out a few minutes later."

10 She had walked for about an hour. When she returned she called out, but no one answered. She searched every room in the house, but couldn't find her husband. Then she thought of the attic. It was horrible! She had cut his body down.

11 The Inspector went up to the attic again. He noted that Hamilton's body had fallen forward, and this must have been the cause of his bruise. As he went out, Black took a last look at the attic door, and around the landing just outside.

????????????????????????????

Black wrote a summary report. Was it suicide or murder?

Chance a clue? **8, 38, 56**

Choose your suspect:
Eloise Hamilton, p.53
Giles Hamilton, p.53
Laurence Hamilton, p.53

INDUSTRIAL ESPIONAGE

Many crimes are committed indoors. In addition to forced entries into private homes and commercial buildings, locked safes are often breached, and not necessarily by force.

1 Stanislaus Pojacksky was a happy man this morning. His design of a silent aeroplane engine had gained the interest of Grievson, Jarrold and Fiske, Ltd., London, a firm of engineers.

2 Ten years of stuffy bed-sitting rooms and grimy toil was over. He'd be Stanislaus Pojacksky, Esq., gentleman of leisure.

3 At 10 o'clock, Pojacksky entered the offices of Grievson, Jarrold and Fiske. He handed his card to Miss Young, Mr. Grievson's private secretary.

4 The inventor was immediately shown into Grievson's room. Grievson listened intently as Pojacksky went over the details of his design.

5 The other two partners, Jarrold and Fiske, were called in to examine the blueprints. The men spent an hour in deep discussion.

6 The three partners then withdrew to the far end of the room. They could hardly contain their excitement — the plan was colossal! "Let's offer him £10,000," whispered Fiske, "and see what he says." The plan was worth far more, but they'd try it.

7 Pojacksky didn't realise the potential value of his plan, so he was very pleased when he persuaded the businessmen to pay him £15,000 for it. Grievson gave the inventor a cheque and even offered him a cigar.

8 "What a day!" declared Grievson as he put the plans into an envelope which he locked up in the safe. "Let's go out and celebrate. The drinks are on me."

9 "Crikey!" Jarrold exclaimed the next morning. He had come in early to start work on the new design. There were papers all over Grievson's desk and the ink pot was overturned. Had someone been there?

The plans! Were they safe?

11 Grievson and Fiske were as upset as Jarrold. This was the worst thing that had ever happened to the firm. Somone in the office must have done it.

10 He rushed to the safe and feverishly spun the dial. The envelope which had contained the plans was empty; another envelope had been opened, but its contents were still intact. The thief had also left something behind. Jarrold was enraged at his insolence. He then phoned his partners, urging them to come to the office straight away.

MANY THANKS

12 Jarrold phoned Scotland Yard. It would take Inspector Black to find the guilty party.

???

To whom does the evidence point?

Chance a clue? **17, 27**

Choose your suspect:
Hamilton Fiske, p.53   *Malcolm Jarrold*, p.54
Daniel Grievson, p.53   *Gwendolyn Young*, p.56

GOING for BROKE

In the majority of cases involving a pistol, the person concerned knows very little about its mechanism. His first shot may be his last.

1 Evelyn Knight, the senior partner of the City firm of Knight and Deay, was still poring over ledgers at nine o'clock one night. The accounts were in a bad state.

2 The junior partner, Howard Deay, sat in an adjoining room writing a letter.

3 Barring the caretaker in the basement, the only other person in the building was Nigel Reeves, one of the clerks, who was reorganizing the files.

4 Just after 9 p.m. Reeves was summoned to Deay's room. The junior partner asked him to slip across the road to post a letter. He was back in ten minutes.

5 Later, Deay entered Reeves' room and asked the clerk to find the file on one of the overdue accounts. "Knight's too easy on them," Deay said. "He should make them pay up."

6 Reeves was just about to locate the file in question when the two young men were suddenly startled by a muffled report from the senior partner's room.

7 Deay ran into Knight's office, followed by Reeves. Evelyn Knight was slumped forward on his desk, a bullet wound in his head. There was a revolver on the floor.

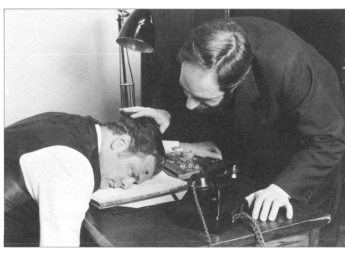

8 Reeves wasted no time. He immediately phoned Scotland Yard to report the death, while the junior partner stayed with the dead man.

9 Inspector Black examined the body. It was not a pretty sight. He noted that the position of the bullet's entry was consistent with suicide — it had penetrated the right temple. He had used a small calibre gun, .22.

10 Then Inspector Black saw a cheque on the desk beneath the dead man's chest. In searching the room, he noted that the electric fire was alight.

11 He stopped to pick up some shreds. There were no scratches or markings of any kind on the desk or the floor.

12 Besides the mysterious shreds and the strong scent of men's cologne, the Inspector found nothing out of the ordinary. He learned that the gun belonged to the dead man and was kept in his desk. Knight had worried about burglars.

13 Inspector Black then listened to the junior partner's details of the events of the evening. Finally, he questioned each man privately, taking careful note of the answers.

?????????????????????????????

The Inspector had his doubts. Was it a case of suicide — or was it murder?

Chance a clue? **7, 47, 55, 62**

Choose your suspect:
Howard Deay, p.53
Evelyn Knight, p.54
Nigel Reeves, p.55

THE BASIL STREET INCIDENT

Whether it is the pocket, kitchen or novelty type, a knife is a threatening instrument. It is readily available, easily concealed, and of great usefulness in the commission of crimes.

1 Kenneth Hoxton loved card games but he hated losing, so he made it a point never to lose. He had recently met a few gambling men and they were due to join him in a private room at his hotel for a quiet game. He glanced around the room with satisfaction. The hotel had even provided flowers.

2 Harry Price, the first visitor, was a young mercenary just back from the Gold Coast and ready for fun.

3 The next man to appear was Arthur Bloom, representative of a firm of shipping agents. He was reputed to be a heavy gambler. Hoxton was an excellent host, and was liberal with the alcohol. Besides, he reasoned, why not get the others in cheery moods before they lost?

That afternoon, Inspector Black, at home with flu, was visited by Sergeant Randall, who told him that Hoxton had been found dead on the floor in a private room at his hotel very early that morning. He had been stabbed. The men who had played cards with him the previous evening had been questioned, but no revealing statements had been made. No fingerprints were found in the room. He was baffled — could the Inspector kindly look at a few photographs he had brought with him?

What the photographs showed

7 The first showed the body. As the men had stayed very late, and most of the guests had gone to bed, no one had heard anything.

8 The second showed the chair in which Hoxton had been seated when he was stabbed. It was obvious that he had dragged himself across the room after having been wounded.

4 They sat down to play as soon as Edmund Seymour, a retired army officer and arms dealer, rushed in. He'd had to work late on an important order.

5 As usual, Hoxton lost for a while. But by ten o'clock he was winning heavily. His guests were no longer cheerful. By midnight, no one but Hoxton was laughing.

6 The men had lost far more than they could afford. Hoxton borrowed a pencil to tot up his winnings. "If I didn't know you better," Price said, "I'd think you cheated."

After the card players left, Hoxton sat down in a large, comfortable chair, loosened his tie, and put his feet up. "Another successful evening," he thought, "but not an awfully good way to make friends. These fellows won't wish to see me again too soon." **But there he was wrong.** One did return that night. . . . A chambermaid found his body the next morning.

---

9 The last picture was of the card table. Randall pointed out the positions of the players. He said that entry had been gained by a french window opening on to a paved yard. No footprints were discernible.

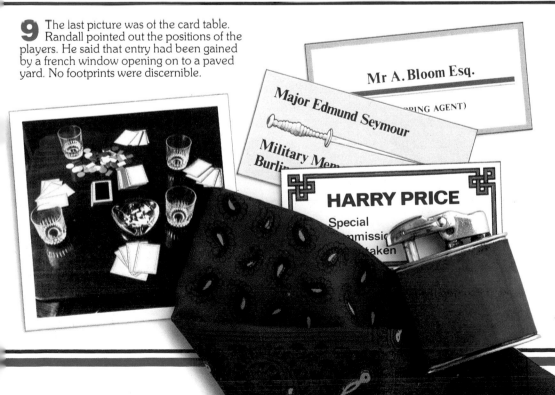

Mr A. Bloom Esq.

(......RING AGENT)

Major Edmund Seymour

Military Mem....
Burli....

HARRY PRICE

Special
....mmissi...
....taken

10 Then Randall brought out the contents of the dead man's pockets — a cigarette lighter and a clean handkerchief. Predictably, Hoxton's wallet had been found empty.

¿ ??????????????????????? ¿

"What do I do next?" young Randall asked the Inspector.
"Arrest your man."
"Which man?" demanded Randall.
"It seems pretty clear to me," said the Inspector.

Is it clear to you?

Chance a clue? **16, 26, 37**

Choose your suspect:
Arthur Bloom, p.52
Harry Price, p.55
Edmund Seymour, p.55

AN END to LIFE

In cases of suspected suicide intent is often inferred from a person's behaviour. However, it also may be established on the basis of an examination of existing evidence.

1 One morning as Miss Moffat was walking downstairs, she smelled gas. She knocked on the door of Mr. Bickerstaff's ground-floor room. There was no answer. She tried to open the door, but it wouldn't budge.

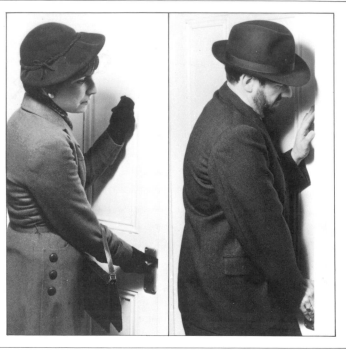

2 Inspector Black was immediately sent for. When he arrived, he too tried the door, but it was stuck fast. Then he shoved hard with his shoulder and burst the door open. He saw at once that it had been sealed along the edges with newspaper.

Too late to save him

3 The Inspector rushed into the room, holding a handkerchief to his face. He opened wide one of the windows. Then he turned off the gas and waited by the door for the air to clear. When he thought it was safe, the Inspector came back and examined Mr. Bickerstaff. He was dead. There was a severe bruise on the back of his head — possibly caused by his falling heavily onto the floor.

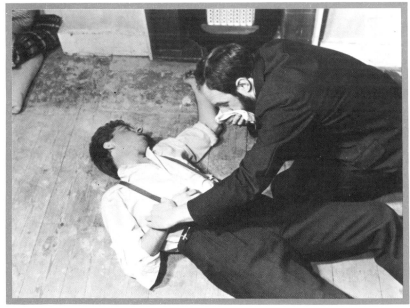

4 Then Inspector Black surveyed the room. At one side was a small table set with a plate, knife, cup, saucer and teaspoon. He noticed that the other window in the room was opened slightly.

5 The only objects on the mantelpiece were a small clock and a pair of leather gloves. A cheap mirror hung above.

6 In the corner next to the fireplace was a pillow and two folded blankets. The Inspector learned that Mr. Bickerstaff had only moved in the day before, and had brought very little with him.

7 Strips of newspaper had been stuck to the door with sealing wax, and four used safety matches were lying on the floor.

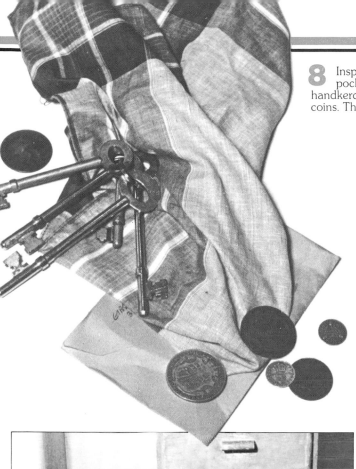

8 Inspector Black emptied the dead man's pockets. They contained a bunch of keys, a handkerchief, three crumpled letters, and a few coins. The contents of the letters were trivial.

9 A closer examination of the table showed that it contained, in addition to the objects already mentioned, a slice of bread, a jam jar, a stick of sealing wax, a coloured pencil and a sheet of the previous day's newspaper, which was opened to the obituary page. Had someone close to Bickerstaff just died?

10 The Inspector opened the small cupboard next to the fireplace and found a plate with a slice of bread, an empty cup and saucer, two empty tins, half a loaf, and tea wrapped in paper. Mr. Bickerstaff had not led a luxurious life.

12 The clock on the mantelpiece had stopped, but the Inspector couldn't say how long ago. The leather gloves seemed just the right size for the dead man. By now, the Inspector had just about completed his investigation.

11 Behind the door hung an overcoat and a scruffy old hat. The pockets of the overcoat contained a few bits of paper, some crumbs of food and three farthings. The print on the old papers was hardly legible, but one piece looked like a bus ticket.

13 Finally, he searched Bickerstaff's shoes, the windows, walls and door for scratches, but didn't find any.

?????????????????????????????
Inspector Black considered for a couple of minutes and then wrote down his suspicions. Was it suicide or murder?

Chance a clue? **6, 31, 46**

Choose your suspect:
Albert Bickerstaff, p.52
Mr. X, p.55

ACCIDENTS DO HAPPEN

The unexpected death of any apparently healthy person is bound to give rise to consideration of the possibility of foul play, however unlikely.

1 "Someone's lying outside — in his pyjamas!" Mrs. Barnsley's speech was fast and loud when she got through to Scotland Yard. She had seen something awful while retrieving her dog from her neighbour's garden. "I thought there was something strange about that Sandhurst. He's been up to no good, you can be sure!"

2 Inspector Black hurried to the Sandhurst mansion. A man had fallen from an upper storey window; his neck appeared to be broken.

3 After several hard knocks, the Inspector managed to rouse Sandhurst who was shocked to see his servant's body. Sandhurst recounted the scene that had greeted him the previous evening. . . .

Mr. Sandhurst's story

4 "I had just returned from a dinner engagement," Sandhurst began, "when I entered the lounge and had a real shock — my trusted servant was lying across the sofa in a drunken stupor! He had gone through half a bottle of my best whiskey." No, he had never caught him at it before, but he had suspected him of being a heavy drinker.

5 "Of course," Sandhurst continued, "I told Jensen that I no longer required his services, but, as it was very late, I would allow him to stay the night. But I'm not even certain he heard what I said, he was so far gone."

6 Since the cook was away, there was no one to help me bring him upstairs. I left him in bed, and returned to my own room."

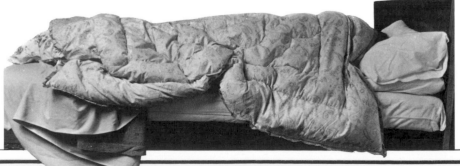

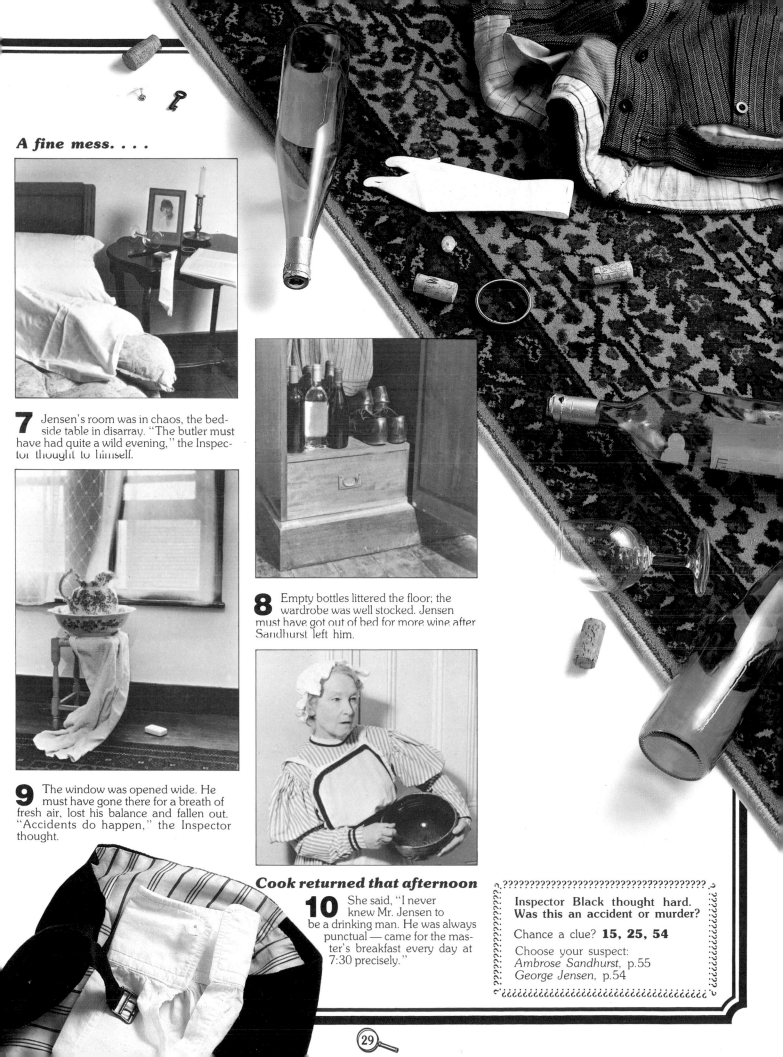

A fine mess. . . .

7 Jensen's room was in chaos, the bedside table in disarray. "The butler must have had quite a wild evening," the Inspector thought to himself.

8 Empty bottles littered the floor; the wardrobe was well stocked. Jensen must have got out of bed for more wine after Sandhurst left him.

9 The window was opened wide. He must have gone there for a breath of fresh air, lost his balance and fallen out. "Accidents do happen," the Inspector thought.

Cook returned that afternoon

10 She said, "I never knew Mr. Jensen to be a drinking man. He was always punctual — came for the master's breakfast every day at 7:30 precisely."

???

Inspector Black thought hard. Was this an accident or murder?

Chance a clue? **15, 25, 54**

Choose your suspect:
Ambrose Sandhurst, p.55
George Jensen, p.54

THEFT at a SEANCE

Not all crimes are premeditated. This one was a spur-of-the-moment decision and hastily improvised. Therefore, the thief left a vital clue.

Inspector H. Black

Criminal Investigation Department
SCOTLAND YARD

2 The card was soon followed by the Inspector himself who listened with sympathy while Mrs. Montague told him about the theft of her pearls.

"One of us is a thief!"

1 This was what Mr. and Mrs. Montague and their three guests were thinking one evening at the Montague's pleasant suburban home. Being under suspicion is not pleasant when you are innocent, and even less so when you are guilty, so that all but one felt relieved when Inspector Black's card appeared.

3 "The pearls were an anniversary gift from my husband. He's a senior partner in a big City firm, you know. I was wearing the pearls for the first time this evening," Mrs. Montague explained.

4 The dinner guests were Mr. Montague's three business associates — two of his partners, Victor Crabtree and Jules Worsthorne — and a member of a Spanish banking house, Señor Carlos Rodriguez. After dinner Mr. Worsthorne, who was interested in psychic matters had suggested holding a séance. "We all thought it a bit of a lark," said Mrs. Montague, "so we agreed to it. He had told us where to sit round the table."

5 "Mr. Worsthorne was on my left, Sr. Rodriguez sat next to him, my husband was on my right, and between Sr. Rodriguez and my husband was Mr. Crabtree. We were told to keep our hands on the table but apart."

7 Someone in the room had taken them. I immediately rang Scotland Yard."

6 "We all sat very still concentrating in the pitch darkness for about twenty minutes," Mrs. Montague continued, "when suddenly I felt a sleeve brush against my shoulder and a hand grab my throat. I screamed. My husband sprang up and turned on the light. My pearls were gone.

Inspector Black investigates

8 The Inspector then examined the room. On reaching the séance table he asked Mr. Montague to point out where everyone had sat. Nothing seemed immediately remarkable.

9 Suddenly Inspector Black noticed something stuck in the back of one of the chairs. It was a cigarette case.

10 Mr. Worsthorne admitted that the case was his and said that he was very absentminded and often left things lying about. The Inspector returned the case to him, and took another quick look round the room. Without any further questioning, Inspector Black asked one of the group to be so kind as to go along with him to the police station.

?????????????????????????

Who stole the pearls?

Chance a clue? **5, 32, 45, 64**

Choose your suspect:
Victor Crabtree, p.52
Phyllis Montague, p.54
Reginald Montague, p.54
Carlos Rodriguez, p.55
Jules Worsthorne, p.56

THE KIDNAPPED BABY

Criminals invariably give themselves away; some are caught by suppressing information they must know, others incriminate themselves by betraying things they should not have known.

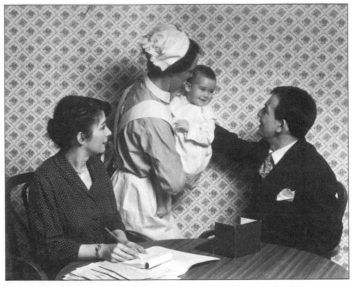

1 Siegfried Elliot was a successful author. His wife had died a year ago, leaving him with a beautiful daughter named Margaret, who was his pride and joy. One evening in July at 6.15 p.m. when Mr. Elliot was busy with his secretary, Miss Dapple, the nurse had brought the baby in as usual to say "good night" and receive her doting father's affectionate kiss.

2 Afterwards the nurse, Miss Woodcock, took the baby upstairs to bed.

Later that night

3 At 10 o'clock that evening, Miss Woodcock heard the baby crying. She went into the nursery and calmed the infant by singing their favourite lullaby. After the nurse left the room in darkness, little Meg was soon sound asleep again.

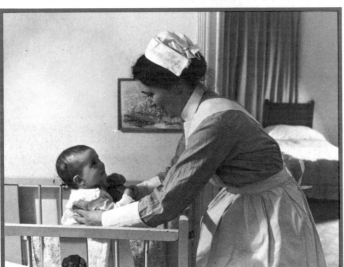

4 At about 11 o'clock, Miss Woodcock retired to bed in one of the rooms leading off the nursery. She did some mending but since she'd had a long day, she soon felt sleepy. She undressed and went to sleep.

6 At 7:30 a.m. a frantic nurse burst into Mr. Elliot's room crying, "The baby! She's gone!" Elliot was horrified. He phoned the police.

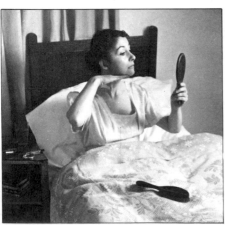

5 About half an hour later, Miss Dapple finished typing out a new chapter and went up to bed herself. At 1:15 a.m., P.C. Carr was passing Mr. Elliot's house when he saw a motorcycle drive off. Was that a white bundle of some sort in the sidecar? He made a note of the time.

7 Inspector Black came round in a police car. He studied the kidnapper's note, which was in the baby's bed.

8,9 It was obvious that the kidnapper had come and left through the window. But the Inspector wondered why no one in the house had heard the baby cry.

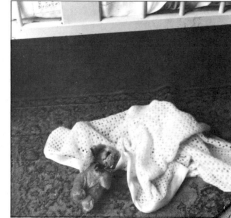

10 He noticed a small bottle on the table just by the bed. Inside were a few drops of chloroform, and some tiny threads of cotton wool round the neck. "So that's why no one heard the baby cry."

11 The kidnapper had certainly done his evil deed in haste. The baby's powder had been spilled all over the rug just beside the bed. A tube of nappy lotion had been crushed.

12 On the side of the bed nearest the window were footprints close together, and a further one beneath the window, all in mud. They were made by the same person. The Inspector recalled that it had rained the previous evening.

The kidnapper's tracks

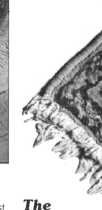

13 When he spoke to Miss Woodcock, she said that she had slept heavily and had heard nothing. If the baby had cried, she would certainly have heard her. She had touched nothing in the room this morning, even leaving on the electric light.

14 Miss Dapple was more helpful. She had woken during the night and heard a motorcycle outside. She sat up in bed. Her luminous watch showed that it was 1:13. She awoke again at 4 a.m., but did not notice anything unusual at either time.

???

Did the kidnapper have inside help? Or was he on his own?

Chance a clue? **14, 24, 53**

Choose your suspect:
Nurse Woodcock, p.56
Edna Dapple, p.52
Mr. X, p.53

MOTIVE for MURDER

Any person with a killer instinct is likely to reach for a blunt instrument, if aroused. Should such a weapon be the nearest one to hand, the consequences are invariably fatal.

1 James Throckmorton, a man of about 60 and a recluse, was known to few except his charlady. One day he wrote a letter to his favourite nephew, William.

2 William was pleased to hear from the old man. But the letter held some shocks. He quickly phoned his brothers.

3 Tom was a clerk in an insurance office. He was hoping for a promotion and had few interests outside his work. He promised to look in.

Laughington
Tuesday

Dear William,
I think it only fair to let you know I am altering my will. I've seen the light and wish to help the wonderful cause of the Heathen Missions.
Since you, Tom and Stephen are young, with plenty of time to earn your fortunes you will not need my few thousands.
Please inform your brothers of my decision.
May God bless you,
Uncle James

4 Stephen was a would-be playwright, who borrowed a few shillings from his brothers whenever he could. That evening the three brothers met at William's small flat. They read their uncle's letter with disappointment and anger. "The old goat has no right to do this to us!" Tom declared. The others agreed.

5 "However," said William, "There's nothing we can do about it now. Let's just hope that the old man gets unconverted again. After all, he's not dead yet."

6 The next evening Throckmorton was reading The Jerusalem Bible when he heard a knock. Being alone, he got up from his chair and admitted his guest himself.

7 The visitor, one of his nephews, made every effort to persuade his uncle to change his will. But the obstinate old man wouldn't budge. Finally, he had enough of being pestered. "Get yourself a drink," he told his nephew, "because you won't get anything else."

8 There Mr. Throckmorton was mistaken. His visitor possessed a temper; grabbing a heavy figurine he moved quickly.

9 One blow was quite enough. It had been, perhaps, unwise of Throckmorton to mention that his will was still unchanged. He had meant to alter it the next day.

At the scene of the crime

11 First he examined the body. Then he took note of the room and all its contents. All fingerprints had been carefully removed from polished surfaces. There were signs of a struggle.

10 The charlady entered the room at 9 o'clock the next morning. She was about to clean the floor, when she saw the body. "God in heaven!" she cried. She left the room without touching anything, and phoned for Inspector Black.

12 There was an evening paper dated from the previous day. The bottom edge was torn through several pages. On closer examination of the page that lay open, the Inspector noticed an "X" near an article about the Church in primitive countries.

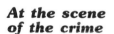

13 The charlady, who described her horror upon finding the body, told the Inspector that the only people Throckmorton ever saw were his nephews — he would never have let anyone else into the house. Later that day the Inspector called in on each nephew for questioning.

???

James Throckmorton lay dead, brutally murdered. Can you identify the guilty nephew, and on what evidence?

Chance a clue? **4, 33, 44**

Choose your suspect:
Stephen Turner, p.56
Thomas Turner, p.56
William Turner, p.56

THE PURLOINED POUNDS

This case took a long time to solve. There wasn't sufficient evidence to arrest anyone. Had an eye-witness been available however, the culprit would have been caught a lot sooner.

1 Every morning Harry Jasper raced to get to work on time. Sometimes he wondered if it was all worth it at £3 a week.

2 James Garnet, another clerk in the same firm, didn't enjoy the rush hour either, but his £2 15s. was sorely needed.

3 The other young worker was Herbert Pearl. He was the newest member of the firm, and only earned £2 12s. 6d.

4 All three men were employed by the rent collecting office of Snatchet and Bleadham. Old man Snatchet insisted on punctuality. Just on 9:30, Pearl was the last to arrive. He rushed into his office and managed to be sitting at his desk when old Snatchet looked round the door. "I can't fine anyone for being late today."

5 At the end of this long day, the three checked the cash box and Jasper, as senior clerk, locked it up and gave Snatchet the key. Snatched growled "goodnight".

6 At home, Jasper studied his law books. He hoped to become a solicitor someday.

7 Garnet, the romanticist, settled down for a relaxing evening with a good novel.

8 Pearl started a long letter to his girl explaining why they'd better postpone their wedding for a year.

9 Lost in complicated crimes and court cases, Jasper read on. "This is impossible!" he despaired, "How much will I remember by tomorrow?"

10 Garnet was in another world with his hero and heroine, who found tragedy and danger round every corner. He would like to write his own masterpiece.

11 Pearl was still writing pages. "It's heart-breaking that we cannot yet be married — if only circumstances were different!" He encouraged his sweetheart to be patient.

During that evening

12 One of the three interrupted his quiet evening at home and paid a visit to the office. He appeared to have had the key to the cash box. In seconds, he had "borrowed" £25.

15 Pearl had written 20 pages. He read them over and was satisfied that he'd explained everything to Cynthia. Will she wait for him?

???

Which clerk was richer by £25?

Chance a clue? **13, 23**

Choose your suspect:
James Garnet, p.53
Harry Jasper, p.54
Herbert Pearl, p.54

¿¿¿

13 Jasper decided that he'd studied enough for one night. He couldn't retain any more facts, so he went to bed.

14 Garnet had finished his novel. Since he'd got a heavy day tomorrow, he decided to go to bed, and blew out the light.

LOCKED ROOM MYSTERY

Like all locked room situations, this has something of the "impossible" about it. But when the impossible has been eliminated, what remains must be the truth, no matter how improbable.

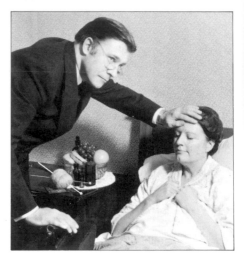

1 Dr. Crumborn had lost a patient — Mrs. Cavendish of "The Bungalow." Something about the case bothered him so he called in at the police station for a chat with his friend, young Police Constable Derek Coombes.

Crumborn's tale

2 He had called to see Mrs. Cavendish about 10 p.m. the previous evening. She had had a severe chest cold, and had been taking an ordinary cough mixture. He had left a bottle of linctus in case the cough became troublesome. As he left, Mrs. Cavendish had asked him to tell the maid she would not be wanted. He had promised to call in early the next morning.

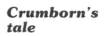

4 A minute later the maid came running in saying she was afraid something had happened. The bedroom door was locked and the key was on the inside. "I knocked and called to the Mistress," she said, "but she didn't answer. Mr. Cavendish has been out since before nine. What should I do?"

3 When he arrived, the maid said she had taken a breakfast tray along as usual, but her mistress seemed to be asleep and her door was locked. He was shown into the study.

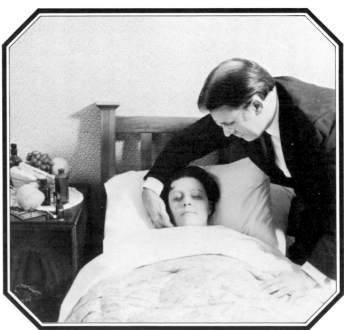

6 Mrs. Cavendish was dead. The appearances suggested morphine poisoning. The linctus he'd left contained a tiny percentage of morphine, but could not account for the symptoms.

7 Beside the bed, however, was a small empty laudanum bottle not there the night before. Some of the linctus had been drunk. "Poor woman," the doctor thought. "Could she have taken the laudanum by accident, or did she have more worries than anyone knew?"

5 Dr. Crumborn did not like to force the door in the husband's absence, but he tried the side window and got in.

Laudanum

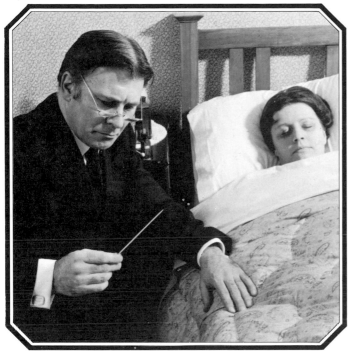

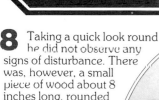

8 Taking a quick look round he did not observe any signs of disturbance. There was, however, a small piece of wood about 8 inches long, rounded and with a point, which he found on the floor

10 The maid informed him that Mr. Cavendish had come in and was now in his study. The doctor went across the hall into the study to meet him and to break the sad news.

9 When he checked the door, he noticed that the lock had recently been oiled.

The key was an old-fashioned type. There were no marks or scratches of any kind on it.

12 Through his sobs, Cavendish went on to say he'd gone to work that morning without awakening his wife to say good-bye.

11 Mr. Cavendish seemed shocked when Dr. Crumborn told him about his wife's death. He said that he had not seen his wife since six o'clock the previous evening. He explained that he had been out to a dinner and it was after midnight when he returned home. Naturally, he had not wished to disturb her, so he slept in the study.

Coombes was puzzled

13 The doctor had emphasised that the window had been securely fastened and the door definitely locked from the inside. He decided to phone Inspector Black for advice.

?????????????????????????

Mrs. Cavendish was dead. Was this suicide, an accident or murder?

Chance a clue? **3, 34, 43, 61, 66**

Choose your suspect:
Nettie, the maid, p.54
Joan Cavendish, p.52
Henry Cavendish, p.52

ROBBERY on the PADDINGTON EXPRESS

The detective's chief proof against law-breakers is the knowledge that fingerprints are unique. Occasionally, even a professional criminal will relax his guard and leave his gloves off and his prints behind.

1 Mr. Elliot Poswaite, of Poswaite and Higginbottom, the prestigious diamond firm, was taking some rare diamonds home for safe-keeping.

4 In the extreme rear compartment was a Mr. Michael Dalston, the younger member of Dalston and Son (Tailors) Ltd. He'd had a trying day, which ended in an argument with Dalston Sr.

2,3 It was Friday night, and, as usual, Poswaite dined in town and caught the 10.15 train to his country home. Poswaite was in the third compartment from the rear of the last coach, which was followed by the guard's van. He sat in the near-side corner, facing the engine. Then he crossed the compartment to open the window, and returned to his seat, settling down for the journey. He soon nodded off.

5 In between Dalston's and Mr. Poswaite's compartments was one occupied by a certain Mr. Ronald Scofield, who was hoping to get some work done during the long ride home. Commuting to London and back every day was wearisome, but he had no other choice — his family had to eat, didn't they?

6 In the compartment just in front of Poswaite's was Geoffrey Rowse. Rowse was an assistant in a big firm of jewellers which often had business dealings with Poswaite's firm. He was thinking about a big transaction he was about to make. "If this works out," he thought, "my troubles will be over, and I will be in clover."

7 As the train was leaving, Dick Purcell ran down the platform into the front compartment of the last coach.

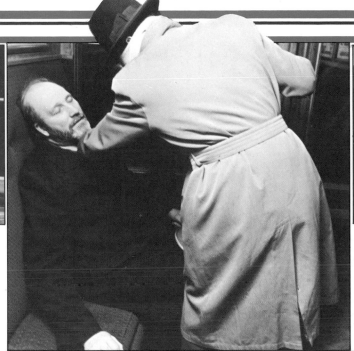

The thief crept in

8 Mr. Poswaite did not see the face looking into his compartment. He'd had a big meal and slept soundly. The rattling of the train drowned out the small noise of the compartment door opening. In seconds, a man was inside.

9 The thief had the diamonds in his hand when Poswaite gave a sudden start. He struggled with the robber, who knocked him unconscious. The robber got away by the same way he had come — along the footboards.

10 When Poswaite came to he managed to stand and pull the emergency cord. When the guard arrived, he told him what had happened. The guard warned all passengers not to leave the train, and phoned the police from a signal box. At the next stop Poswaite told his story to Inspector Black.

11 Mr. Poswaite was shaken by his terrifying experience. "And the next thing I knew," he explained, "the compartment was spinning round and my priceless diamonds were gone!"

12 When the Inspector examined the compartment, he paid particular attention to the inside of the off-side door, where he found some fingerprints. Then he talked to the guard, and discovered that this was the first run the train had made since receiving a thorough wash-down that morning.

13 Inspector Black called together the four men who had occupied Mr. Poswaite's coach, and questioned them in the station waiting room. Three continued their journeys.

?????????????????????????????
One man's fingerprints matched those on the train. He also had the gems in his specially-constructed pockets. **Who was guilty?**

Chance a clue? **12, 22, 51**

Choose your suspect:
Michael Dalston, p.52
Dick Purcell, p.55
Geoffrey Rowse, p.55
Ronald Scofield, p.55
?????????????????????????????

DIAMONDS AREN'T FOREVER

One of the commonest motives for murder is greed. The most likely victim is well-to-do but not particularly generous. He or she has something that another person wants, and, if necessary, may have to be eliminated in order to part company with the desired object.

1 Wilfred Barnes Quackenbush, coin and gem collector, lived alone on a large estate in Surrey. He was not known to have any enemies. Recently he had acquired something that was the envy of many — the Cape Diamond. Quackenbush often examined the diamond in the morning light, and left it lying on his desk in the study. He knew that Jeffers, the gardener, occasionally stopped his work to steal a peek at it.

2 One day he had a visit from his neighbour who was a connoisseur of gems. It was near tea-time when Hoskins entered the study with his card.

3 Quackenbush closed the shutters and adjusted the light to show off the gem's sparkling brilliance.

4 Archibald Peregrin dropped his usual dignified calm when he beheld the diamond. "Simply perfection!" he enthused. "You've certainly out-done yourself this time, old chap!"

5 Soon after it was Hoskins' day off, and he went to the village for tea with his friend, Vincent, a footman at another country house. Hoskins told him about his master's beautiful new diamond.

6 Jeffers, who appreciated things of great beauty, was very excited about the gem. He told Higgins, the pedlar, all about it over a drink. Higgins had been in gaol for burglary several years earlier.

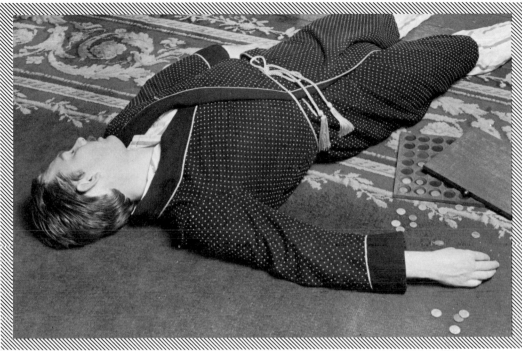

7 A few nights later, Quackenbush, upstairs in bed, heard a noise. He went down and saw a thief at his safe. That was the last thing he ever saw.

8 Hoskins found the body the next morning, lying among the coins the man had so cherished. The diamond was gone. Hoskins rushed to the phone to call the police.

9,10,11 The Inspector arrived and asked Hoskins about the people who would have seen the diamond. Jeffers insisted that although he had told Higgins about the diamond no one had overheard them. Then the Inspector summoned Peregrin who admitted that although he had never seen a finer gem he wouldn't have risked his reputation by stealing it.

12 At the police station, Higgins was nervous. He insisted he had told no one about the gem.

13 Finally, Inspector Black saw Vincent, and asked him a few leading questions.

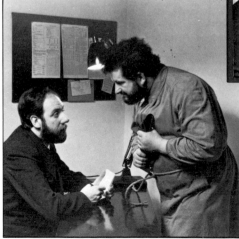

????????????????????????????????

Who stole the diamond?

Chance a clue? **2, 35, 42**

Choose your suspect:
Peter Vincent, p.56
Sid Higgins, p.53
Horace Hoskins, p.54
Bob Jeffers, p.54
Archibald Peregrin, p.55

BLACK on the BEAT

The opportunity to commit murder depends entirely on a few key elements. These are, firstly, favourable circumstances; secondly, timing; and lastly, a certain amount of luck on the murderer's part. This case contained all three.

1 Inspector Henry Black was late coming home one night when he heard a strange sound. He rushed up, and found a girl lying in the road beside her scattered belongings. A man ran off as he approached. The Inspector recognised Miss Danbery, the daughter of a local politician.

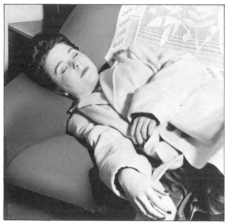

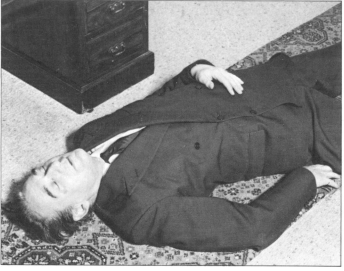

2 Black carried the girl to the door of her nearby home. A man who introduced himself as David Tavistock, Danbery's secretary, led the Inspector into the sitting room and told him that Mr. Danbery had been fatally attacked in his study.

3 Inspector Black left the unconscious girl lying on the settee with Tavistock looking after her while he found the study.

4 Danbery was lying on the rug in the middle of the room. He had been killed by a heavy blow on the head. The window was wide open.

Tavistock's evidence

5 The Inspector took a good look round the outside of the house. Just beneath the study window were two footprints leading away from the house. There was nothing else out of the ordinary in the garden. He returned to the sitting room to question the secretary.

6 He said that he hadn't seen Danbery in the hour prior to finding him, but that he'd had an appointment to see him in the study at 9:30.

7 When he came in at 9:30, he saw his employer on the floor, and a man escaping through the window.

Miss Danbery's story

8 Miss Danbery now seemed well enough to talk. She told the Inspector that she had seen her father just after dinner that evening in his study.

9 He was angry and upset. "He was muttering something like, 'The bounder! He can't forge my name and get away with it!' I begged him to tell me what was wrong," Miss Danbery sobbed, "but he wouldn't."

10 "He never discussed anything with me," she complained. "He always treated me like a child." Mr. Danbery had given her a letter to post. "I was surprised that it was addressed to my uncle, Superintendent Peters, at Stow-on-the-Wold," she said.

12 Around 9:15 she put on her coat and went out to the pillar box. Yes, the letter was still in her pocket.

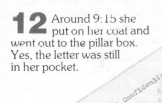

Private and Confidential
Superintendent of Police
The Police Station
Stow-on-the-Wold
Gloucestershire

11 "Father told me to ask Tavistock to see him at 9:30," the girl added. "It was 8:15 then. I went to my room and read for an hour."

13 After the Inspector read the letter, which was a request for the Superintendent to call in the following day, he asked Miss Danbery if her father had had any enemies. "Not to my knowledge," she replied.
"Mr. Tavistock?"
"Well, I haven't been with Mr. Danbery very long," he said, "but I have gathered that there had been some unpleasantness with a business partner."

????????????????????????????
Who killed Danbery?
A stranger or a business partner?
A member of the household?

Chance a clue? **11, 21, 58**

Choose your suspect:
David Tavistock, p.56
Mr. X, p.52

THE PARK LANE AFFAIR

A good investigator can make his recognition of physical evidence more sophisticated only through education and experience. He should, at all times, differentiate between what is vital and what isn't.

1 On Isabel Calbert's first day in London she got ready to go to the museums and galleries she had heard so much about. She had been looking forward to this holiday for a long time.

2 Henrietta had been just as excited about coming to London as her twin. Even close friends of the girls had difficulty in telling them apart — especially when they dressed alike. The sisters hoped to enhance their wardrobe by shopping in the big stores.

3 The twins spent the early part of the morning in the National Gallery, and then went to the shops in Oxford Street. They returned to the hotel at midday to leave their purchases. After a brief rest, they went out again, and spent the rest of the day sightseeing.

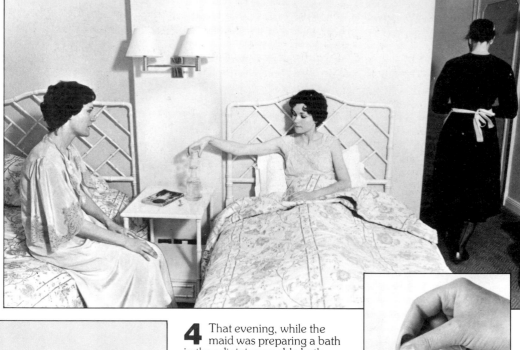

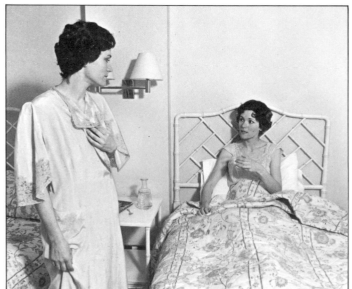

4 That evening, while the maid was preparing a bath in the adjoining marble bathroom, Henrietta complained of a headache. "Have you got any aspirin, Isabel?" she said. There was water by the bed. She helped herself to some and stirred the aspirin in it.

5 "I think I'll have dinner sent up to the room," said Henrietta. Isabel offered to keep her sister company for the evening, and suggested that two dinner trays should be sent up. But Henrietta wouldn't hear of it.

7 When the maid brought the dinner tray in, she was surprised to find the room empty. When she looked into the bathroom, she was horrified! She quickly pulled the bath plug out and ran downstairs for help. **But no one could be of much help now.**

6 Later on, the head waiter in the Louis Room Restaurant received instructions to send up a light dinner for one to Room 12. The other sister dined downstairs.

8 The hotel doctor tried artificial respiration, but it was too late. There was no sign of injury to her body or indication how she'd slipped and stunned herself. He gave orders that the dead girl's sister, who was dining downstairs, was not to be admitted.

9 Worried, the doctor alerted the police. First on the scene was a local bobby followed shortly by Inspector Black. The first step was to test the glass for fingerprints.

10 Then Inspector Black began an investigation of the bathroom. The pockets of the girl's silk dressing gown were empty.

11 The constable returned. The tumbler showed only the dead girl's prints.

12 The hotel doctor confirmed that the tumbler had contained aspirin and nothing else. Inspector Black carried the body into the bedroom and sent the constable for the girl's sister. Meanwhile, he questioned the maid, who was visibly shaken. He learned what he could about the twins and exactly what the maid had observed before dinner. He was satisfied they had had no visitors.

13 Suddenly the door flung open. An agonised cry of "Henrietta!" filled the room. The sister ran to the bed and stood over the body, staring in disbelief. The Inspector was astonished at the striking resemblance between the sisters.

14 Then the girl burst into uncontrollable sobs. The Inspector told the constable to take her into another suite.

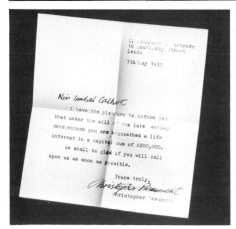

15 When they had gone, the Inspector stooped down to pick up the handbag which the girl had dropped as she ran to the bed. In it was a letter.

16 "No motive there," the Inspector thought. He returned to the bathroom and noticed something — a watch engraved with the initials H.C. and a ring. He recalled that the sister had cried "Henrietta!" when she ran into the room.

17 Back in the bedroom once again, Inspector Black noticed a brown leather handbag bearing the same initials as the watch on the armchair. He thought he'd better check the contents.

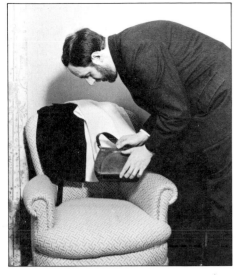

18 He had just tipped out everything in the bag when the constable interrupted. "Miss Calbert seems calm enough to answer a few questions now, Inspector," he said.

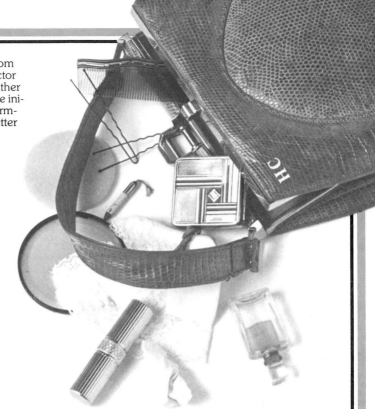

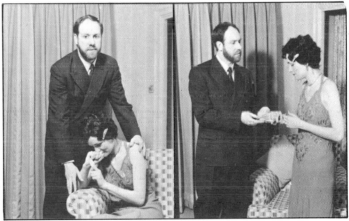

19 The bereaved sister said that she had last seen Henrietta before going down to dinner. Her sister was just entering the bathroom. Inspector Black returned her evening bag and said he might ask her a few more questions later on.

20 The Inspector saw that the younger man was examining a screw of paper. He seemed to remember having seen it before. "What have you got there, Constable?" he said. The constable opened his hand and revealed the contents of the paper.

21 The white tablets looked like ordinary aspirin, but a good detective never takes anything for granted. The Inspector tasted one of the tablets cautiously. "Aspirin," he confirmed.

???????????????????????????
Was Black convinced that this was an accident? Was it suicide? Or was it murder?

Chance a clue? **1, 36, 41, 50**

Choose your suspect:
Henrietta Calbert, p.52
Isabel Calbert, p.52

THE CLUES

?1

See picture 4.
Is this clue hard to swallow?
Lose 10 points.

?2

Did he spread it thin?
Lose 10 points.

?3

The plot's unravelling.
Lose 10 points.

?4

A man's best friend?
Lose 15 points.

?5

Powdered shoulders were
all the rage.
Lose 15 points.

?6

A strike against you if you
can't solve this one.
Lose 15 points.

?7

Put these together and
what do you get?
Lose 15 points.

?8

Was he really at the end of
his tether?
Lose 20 points.

?9

"Out, damned spot!"
Lose 20 points.

?10

See picture 11.
Not up to scratch.
Lose 20 points.

?11

A regular correspondence?
Lose 10 points.

?12

Printed proof.
Lose 10 points.

?13

Did Garnet burn his candle
at both ends?
Lose 15 points.

?14

Something wicked came
this way. Lose 15 points.

?15

He sure drank it neat!
Lose 15 points.

?16

If you're having a stab at
the dagger, it's a red herring. Lose 20 points.

?17

A clear-cut clue?
Lose 15 points.

?18

Who pays the piper?
Lose 20 points.

?19

I've seen this somewhere
before. Lose 20 points.

?20

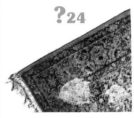

A shot in the dark?
Lose 20 points.

?21

Making tracks . . .
Lose 10 points.

?22

A cover-up?
Lose 10 points.

?23

Time is of the essence.
Lose 15 points.

?24

A step in the right direction?
Lose 15 points.

?25

Was alcohol his undoing?
Lose 15 points.

?26

"A rose by any other
name . . ." Lose 15 points.

?27

Clue for a sharp detective.
Lose 15 points.

?28

A hair-raising experience?
Lose 20 points.

?29

The murderer's no stick-in-
the-mud. Are you?
Lose 20 points.

?30

A token of affection? No, a
red herring. Lose 20 points.

?31

The Inspector could find no
scratches on the walls or
the dead man's shoes. Why
was he looking for them?
Lose 15 points.

?32

Don't let smoke get in your
eyes. Lose 15 points.

?33

Has your theory gone up in
smoke? Lose 15 points.

?34

More than meets the eye?
Lose 10 points.

?35

All that glitters . . .
Lose 10 points.

?36

A stiff drink.
Lose 10 points.

?37

See picture 6.
Neither a borrower, nor a
lender be. Lose 15 points.

?38

Does a hanged man gather
dust? Lose 20 points.

?39

A spotless reputation?
Lose 20 points.

?40

A sizable clue.
Lose 20 points.

?41

The last grasp.
Lose 10 points.

?42

A stab in the dark . . .
Lose 10 points.

?43

The key to the problem . . .
Lose 10 points.

?44

No news is . . . a red herring. Lose 20 points.

?45

This party had its ups and
downs. Lose 15 points.

?46

This cupboard wasn't bare.
Lose 15 points.

?47

Money talks.
Lose 15 points.

?48

You blew this one! Red
herring. Lose 20 points.

?49

Was it something Miss
Peattie said?
Lose 20 points.

?50

Have you got the case all
wrapped up?
Lose 10 points.

?51

Hard to handle?
Lose 10 points.

?52

Put the right foot forward.
Lose 20 points.

?53

Did Miss Dapple have a
room with a view?
Lose 15 points.

?54

As a clue, this doesn't hold
water. Red herring.
Lose 20 points.

?55

A timely clue.
Lose 15 points.

?56

What a drag.
Lose 20 points.

?57

A love letter, but not sealed
with a kiss.
Lose 20 points.

?58

Letter-perfect?
Lose 10 points.

?59

Picture this?
Lose 20 points.

?60

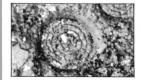

A tell-tale mark.
Lose 20 points.

?61

Pocket full of why?
Lose 10 points.

?62

Hot on the trail.
Lose 15 points.

?63

He'd been hurt in more
ways than one.
Lose 20 points.

?64

Cigarettes are damaging to
your solution. Red herring.
Lose 20 points.

?65

It was George Halliday's
hat and his hair. Red herring. Lose 20 points.

?66

See picture 9.
Oil's well that ends well?
Lose 10 points.

?67

No marks for penmanship.
Lose 20 points.

THE SUSPECTS

Was there a clue in his pockets?

Yes **1**   No **2**

Had he had company before he died?

Yes **3**   No **4**

Ans. **H** ....

ALBERT BICKERSTAFF

Was there something unusual about the tumbler?

Yes **5**   No **6**

Was she identical to her sister?

Yes **7**   No **8**

Ans. **B** ....

ISABEL CALBERT

Was it significant that she asked that the maid not disturb her?

Yes **5**   No **6**

Did she appear to be in great pain or distress?

Yes **7**   No **8**

Ans. **I** ....

JOAN CAVENDISH

Did she tell the truth about not seeing anything unusual?

Yes **1**   No **2**

Did she have easy access to the baby's room?

Yes **3**   No **4**

Ans. **D** ....

EDNA DAPPLE

Did he leave his pencil with Hoxton?

Yes **1**   No **2**

Did Hoxton identify him in any way?

Yes **3**   No **4**

Ans. **A** ....

ARTHUR BLOOM

Is there something peculiar about his walking stick?

Yes **1**   No **2**

Was there a link between his stick and the other evidence?

Yes **3**   No **4**

Ans. **P** ....

PERCY CARRINGTON

Was there more than one piece of evidence which implicated him?

Yes **1**   No **2**

Was his position at the séance table significant?

Yes **3**   No **4**

Ans. **R** ....

VICTOR CRABTREE

Could he have known about the letter?

Yes **5**   No **6**

Would a business associate have to attack Miss Danbery as well?

Yes **7**   No **8**

Ans. **F** ....

MR. X

Could she have slipped in the bath and stunned herself?

Yes **1**   No **2**

Had she had something unusual in her handbag?

Yes **3**   No **4**

Ans. **B** ....

HENRIETTA CALBERT

Had he lied about seeing his wife that evening?

Yes **1**   No **2**

Is there any way he could have committed the crime and left the room locked up?

Yes **3**   No **4**

Ans. **I** ....

HENRY CAVENDISH

Does his being left-handed have any bearing on the case?

Yes **1**   No **2**

Is his position on the train inconsistent with the fingerprints?

Yes **3**   No **4**

Ans. **S** ....

MICHAEL DALSTON

Had she shot herself elsewhere and been moved to the bed?

Yes **1**   No **2**

Could she have had a disagreement with her husband?

Yes **3**   No **4**

Ans. **J** ....

CLARISSA DAVENPORT

Was his story about the letter substantiated?

Yes **5**   No **6**

Had he made any changes to the room while Inspector Black was telephoning?

Yes **7**   No **8**

Ans. **J** ....

GERALD DAVENPORT

Could you prove that he was reading his novel the entire evening?

Yes **1**   No **2**

Did he have further to travel than his colleagues?

Yes **3**   No **4**

Ans. **M** ....

JAMES GARNET

Would he have told his partners about the plans if he was going to steal them?

Yes **5**   No **6**

Was his suggestion of celebrating suspicious?

Yes **7**   No **8**

Ans. **Q** ....

DANIEL GRIEVSON

Did he have a motive for wanting his brother dead?

Yes **9**   No **10**

Was he capable of murdering his brother and making it look like suicide?

Yes **11**   No **12**

Ans. **N** ....

LAURENCE HAMILTON

Could his asking Reeves to post a letter be considered a coincidence?

Yes **1**   No **2**

Did the mysterious "shreds" belong to Knight?

Yes **3**   No **4**

Ans. **O** ....

HOWARD DEAY

Does his violent temper make him a prime suspect?

Yes **1**   No **2**

Would you expect to find his fingerprints on the gun?

Yes **3**   No **4**

Ans. **C** ....

WALLACE GOODHEW

Do you think she wanted her husband "out of the way?"

Yes **1**   No **2**

Was she capable of murdering her husband alone and making it appear to be suicide?

Yes **3**   No **4**

Ans. **N** ....

ELOISE HAMILTON

Does his previous gaol sentence have any bearing on the case?

Yes **1**   No **2**

Is there any evidence against him?

Yes **3**   No **4**

Ans. **K** ....

SID HIGGINS

Did he know the safe's combination?

Yes **1**   No **2**

Did he know in which envelope the plans were?

Yes **3**   No **4**

Ans. **Q** ....

HAMILTON FISKE

Was there something peculiar about his footprints?

Yes **9**   No **10**

Had someone handed him the baby?

Yes **11**   No **12**

Ans. **D** ....

MR. X

Was there something peculiar about his glasses?

Yes **5**   No **6**

Is there anything strange about his wound?

Yes **7**   No **8**

Ans. **N** ....

GILES HAMILTON

Did Hodgson make a revealing statement?

Yes **1**   No **2**

Is Hodgson wearing anything that would link him to the chair?

Yes **3**   No **4**

Ans. **G** ....

JOHN HODGSON

Could he have chosen a more opportune time to steal the diamond?

Yes **5**   No **6**

Would he have talked about it if he meant to steal it?

Yes **7**   No **8**

Ans. **K** ....

HORACE HOSKINS

Did Jeffers have an opportunity to steal the diamond?

Yes **9**   No **10**

Would he have mentioned it to his friend if he were going to steal it?

Yes **11**   No **12**

Ans. **K** ....

BOB JEFFERS

Was this a hot day?

Yes **5**   No **6**

Was there anything in his behaviour that wasn't consistent with suicide?

Yes **7**   No **8**

Ans. **O** ....

EVELYN KNIGHT

Would he steal the pearls for the insurance money?

Yes **9**   No **10**

Did he want to throw suspicion on one of his associates?

Yes **11**   No **12**

Ans. **R** ....

REGINALD MONTAGUE

Did he see the envelope that the plans were in?

Yes **13**   No **14**

If he stole the plans, would he have phoned the police?

Yes **15**   No **16**

Ans. **Q** ....

MALCOLM JARROLD

Was the evidence in Jensen's room consistent with his being a heavy drinker?

Yes **1**   No **2**

Was it proven that he drank heavily?

Yes **3**   No **4**

Ans. **E** ....

GEORGE JENSEN

Did he have a strong motive for murdering Marks?

Yes **5**   No **6**

Does anything on the dead man's desk point to him?

Yes **7**   No **8**

Ans. **C** ....

GODFREY MILLER

Would Pearl risk losing his job in order to marry Cynthia?

Yes **9**   No **10**

Could he have written a 20-page letter *and* stolen the money?

Yes **11**   No **12**

Ans. **M** ....

HERBERT PEARL

Would Jasper jeopardise his law career by committing a crime?

Yes **5**   No **6**

Would his "alibi" let him off?

Yes **7**   No **8**

Ans. **M** ....

HARRY JASPER

Is there any indication she saw her mistress later that night?

Yes **9**   No **10**

Is there any reason to suspect she lied about her mistress not answering?

Yes **11**   No **12**

Ans. **I** ....

NETTIE JONES

Do you think the pearls were insured?

Yes **5**   No **6**

Do you think she had enough housekeeping money?

Yes **7**   No **8**

Ans. **R** ....

PHYLLIS MONTAGUE

Did anything on the dead man's desk point specifically to her?

Yes **9**   No **10**

Was her testimony revealing?

Yes **11**   No **12**

Ans. **C** ....

GRACE PEATTIE

Was Peck's handkerchief definite proof that he was guilty of murder?

Yes **1**   No **2**

Was there something remarkable about his handkerchief?

Yes **3**   No **4**

Ans. **L** ....

TED PECK

Is the fact that he was the last to board the train significant?

Yes **5**   No **6**

Would you consider his athletic build important to the case?

Yes **7**   No **8**

Ans. **S** ....

DICK PURCELL

Was he a suspicious type?

Yes **13**   No **14**

Could he claim diplomatic immunity?

Yes **15**   No **16**

Ans. **R** ....

CARLOS RODRIGUEZ

Was he sitting in a position to have done the robbery?

Yes **13**   No **14**

Is there anything about his appearance that might be of relevance to the case?

Yes **15**   No **16**

Ans. **S** ....

RONALD SCOFIELD

Was he openly jealous of Quackenbush?

Yes **13**   No **14**

Would he have been able to dispose of the stone easily?

Yes **15**   No **16**

Ans. **K** ....

ARCHIBALD PEREGRIN

Did Quigley have an opportunity to commit the crime?

Yes **5**   No **6**

Did he give the impression of being innocent?

Yes **7**   No **8**

Ans. **L** ....

SAMUEL QUIGLEY

Did his position on the train put him under suspicion?

Yes **9**   No **10**

Would he have known that Poswaite was carrying valuable stones this evening?

Yes **11**   No **12**

Ans. **S** ....

GEOFFREY ROWSE

Does his position at the table have any bearing on the case?

Yes **9**   No **10**

Would he have difficulty getting a knife?

Yes **11**   No **12**

Ans. **A** ....

EDMUND SEYMOUR

Did he believe his host was honest?

Yes **5**   No **6**

Did he appear to be a suspicious character?

Yes **7**   No **8**

Ans. **A** ....

HARRY PRICE

Could he have posted the letter and still have had time to kill Knight?

Yes **9**   No **10**

Did he give the Inspector any significant information?

Yes **11**   No **12**

Ans. **O** ....

NIGEL REEVES

Did he tell Inspector Black the whole truth about Jensen?

Yes **5**   No **6**

Were there signs he had deliberately arranged Jensen's room?

Yes **7**   No **8**

Ans. **E** ....

AMBROSE SANDHURST

Had he covered all his tracks?

Yes **5**   No **6**

Had he remembered to leave something important behind?

Yes **7**   No **8**

Ans. **H** ....

MR. X

Did he wash his hands after writing the suicide note?

Yes **9**   No **10**

Is the fact that he had been drinking from a teacup of any significance?

Yes **1'1**   No **12**

Ans. **L** ....,

HAROLD SIMMONDS

Could he have known about the letter?

Yes **1**   No **2**

Could he have manufactured all the evidence?

Yes **3**   No **4**

Ans. **F** ....

DAVID TAVISTOCK

Was he bluffing when he said "There's nothing we can do about it"?

Yes **9**   No **10**

Would the favoured nephew have the strongest motive?

Yes **11**   No **12**

Ans. **T** ....

WILLIAM TURNER

Was it reasonable that she could have slept heavily?

Yes **5**   No **6**

Is there any evidence that she put on the electric light?

Yes **7**   No **8**

Ans. **D** ....

NURSE WOODCOCK

Was there a link between Steinmetz and the scratch on the chair?

Yes **5**   No **6**

Did Steinmetz look like a thief?

Yes **7**   No **8**

Ans. **G** ....

ROBIN STEINMETZ

Was it apparent he had less money than the others?

Yes **1**   No **2**

Did he appear to have a "hot" temper?

Yes **3**   No **4**

Ans. **T** ....

STEPHEN TURNER

Was he physically equipped to have murdered Quackenbush?

Yes **17**   No **18**

Had he left anything at the scene?

Yes **19**   No **20**

Ans. **K** ....

PETER VINCENT

Was his statement about the cigarette case convincing?

Yes **17**   No **18**

Is it significant that he suggested the séance, with the hands held apart?

Yes **19**   No **20**

Ans. **R** ....

JULES WORSTHORNE

Did Sykes' muddy boots have any bearing on the crime?

Yes **5**   No **6**

Did the Inspector have any reason to doubt his alibi?

Yes **7**   No **8**

Ans. **P** ....

PHILLIP SYKES

Were his smoking habits different from his brothers?

Yes **5**   No **6**

Was there a direct link between him and the murdered man?

Yes **7**   No **8**

Ans. **T** ....

THOMAS TURNER

Might he have stolen the painting to raise some cash?

Yes **9**   No **10**

Do you think Waverly will inherit more money in time?

Yes **11**   No **12**

Ans. **G** ....

TIM WAVERLY

Was there something peculiar about the envelopes that had been tampered with?

Yes **9**   No **10**

Did she know which envelope held the plans?

Yes **11**   No **12**

Ans. **Q** ....

GWENDOLYN YOUNG

THE EVIDENCE

13

A Hoxton didn't put it in writing! Lose 10 points.

B You've misinterpreted one part of the evidence. See clue 41 and lose 25 points.

C No more of a suspect than the others and if you expected to see his prints you'd be disappointed. Lose 25 points.

D If this is the case, nothing's proved. But you've missed some hard evidence. See clue 53 and lose 10 points.

E Careful study of text and pictures would demonstrate you are mistaken. Lose 30 points.

F Nobody better, though he got some things wrong. Award yourself 200 points and read the Truth, p.61.

G Thieves rarely let their intentions slip, and there's no link with the chair. Lose 30 points.

H One good clue, one red herring. Lose 25 points.

I Congratulations! If you've worked out how this one was done you're a credit to the force. Award yourself 200 points and read the Truth, p. 62.

J If you agree, then you'll agree it was no suicide. Lose 25 points.

K Poor chap. Relegated to suspect status on circumstantial evidence only. Lose 30 points.

L These answers cancel each other out. Check clue 67, lose 25 points, and try again.

M I don't think you could "prove" anything! See clue 13 or 23 if you don't believe me. Lose 20 points.

N Well, she would have needed some help. Try again and lose 10 points.

O A confusing answer. You haven't thought this one through. Lose 10 points.

P Full marks for your observations! Award yourself 100 points and read the Truth on p.61.

Q He wouldn't have acted with hesitation, then. You've chosen too quickly. Lose 20 points.

R Close, but not close enough. Try again and lose 10 points.

S You've missed your train. A glance at clue 12 may put you on the right track. Lose 20 points.

T There isn't any real evidence for either answer. Lose 30 points.

14

A You've missed an important clue. Check clue 26 and lose 20 points.

B You think it's an accident; but check clue 50 and lose 30 points.

C You're right, so that you should point you in a different direction. See clue 30 and lose 20 points.

D You haven't studied the case carefully enough. Lose 20 points.

E Seems as though the evidence has been too neatly arranged. Lose 25 points.

F Not a reasonable answer! Check clue 11 or 21. Lose 10 points.

G Somebody else is more worthy of suspicion. See clue 52 and lose 25 points.

H You're seeing things in the wrong places. Lose 30 points.

I You've missed vital evidence. Check clue 34 or 43 and lose 10 points.

J Then why was her body moved? Check clue 28 or 18 and try again. Lose 30 points.

K A previous gaol sentence doesn't prove guilt. Lose 25 points.

L You've missed the significance of the evidence. Check clues 39 and 67, lose 30 points, and try again.

M You've missed an important clue! See clue 13 and think again. Lose 10 points.

N You're right. She's not entirely innocent but not wholly guilty. Award yourself 50 points and see if you can get the rest before reading the Truth on p.61.

O You've missed the real significance of this case. Check clue 47 and lose 20 points.

23

A You were right to bet on Bloom; he sure was guilty! Award yourself 150 points and read the Truth, p.60.

B Yes, it seems obvious this wasn't an accident. Lose 20 points.

C He's a good actor — he fooled you, didn't he? He's not the one. Lose 30 points.

D She lied about something, and that was her part in this play. Award yourself 75 points if you knew she had been involved and read the Truth, p.60.

E An inconsistent answer which won't give you the solution. Lose 25 points.

F He'd have had to know about the letter to do the rest. Lose 10 points.

G Can't see it myself — someone else looks more suspicious. See clue 52 and lose 25 points.

H You're right, so this looks like murder, not suicide. Lose 20 points.

I Your answers conflict. Lose 10 points.

J You missed a good clue. Check clue 59 and lose 20 points.

K Do you know something I don't know? See clue 35 or 42 and lose 25 points.

L That means he wasn't guilty. Lose 20 points and try again.

M You're part-way there, but you've got to watch yourself. See clue 23 and try again. Lose 10 points.

N Can you think of any reason why she'd want him around? Lose 20 points.

O No, it wasn't a mere coincidence. Award yourself 150 points and read the Truth, p.62.

P I think you've just made a guess. Proper reasoning is the essence of good detective work. Lose 10 points.

Q One piece of information wouldn't have been much use without the other. Lose 25 points.

R Wrong answers, but keep your spirits up. Try again and lose 20 points.

S Left-handed, right-handed, it's his position on the train that's important. Try clue 51 — it may shed some light. Lose 10 points.

T His temper was no more proved than his finances. Lose 25 points.

24

A Half right, but you've missed the incriminating clue. Check clue 26 and lose 10 points.

B Check clue 50 and try again. Lose 25 points.

C Then why question him at all — are you starstruck? Lose 25 points.

D Better study the story again. Lose 10 points.

E You're right to doubt this evidence, and therefore you should doubt his "accident". Lose 20 points.

F You're more confused than the recuperating Miss Danbery! Lose 20 points.

G Have you anything else to go on? Perhaps a clue would be in order. See clue 52 and lose 20 points.

H You're not fooled by red herrings, or actual evidence, either. Lose 25 points.

I The evidence is before you but you choose not to see it. Check clue 61 and lose 20 points.

J Too many suspicious factors about this case to let it go at suicide. Lose 25 points.

K Not much of a suspect. Lose 20 points.

L This is evidence which exonerates him. Check clue 67, lose 25 points and try again.

M There's definite proof he didn't read all evening and since he lives closest to the office, he's the likely lad. Award yourself 150 points.

N She's not as innocent as she looks. Check the story again. Lose 10 points.

O Only half right; what bearing do the "shreds" have on the case. Lose 10 points.

P Even an amateur would feel there was something suspicious about a muddy walking stick with a clean tip, to say nothing about its connection with the rest of the evidence. No marks for good detection here. Lose 20 points.

Q It seems as though you know less than he did! Lose 30 points.

R Right man, but not enough proof. Try again and lose 10 points.

S Left-handed or not, he's the man. Award yourself 200 points and read the Truth, p.61.

T Not much of a suspect. Check clue 33 for real evidence. Lose 20 points.

57

A I wouldn't gamble on you as a detective. Lose 30 points.

B You're part-way there. Check clue 50 and lose 10 points.

C No stronger than any of the others and perhaps the so-called evidence was a simple coincidence. Lose 25 points.

D You're looking for answers where there aren't any. Lose 25 points.

E Why rearrange Jensen's room unless to support a story or a lie? Lose 10 points.

F Seems a lot to ask of a relative stranger. Lose 30 points.

G You're right and it's not plain prejudice! Read the Truth, p.62, and award yourself 100 points.

H You've missed some important things. Check clues 46 and 31 and lose 30 points.

I Neither answer is correct. Lose 30 points.

J If he made changes to the room, he certainly could have lied. Lose 10 points.

K Your answers conflict. Lose 25 points.

L Opportunity counts, but you've missed an important clue. Lose 10 points.

M I don't think you're a good judge of character, but even if he had a motive, he hasn't got the opportunity. Check clue 23 and lose 25 points.

N Both indicate this was murder and not suicide. Lose 20 points.

O You're right on both counts so this looks like murder, not suicide. Lose 20 points.

P You obviously think Sykes did it. But isn't your evidence just circumstantial? You ought to check clue 19 or 29. Lose 30 points.

Q Most criminals aren't that clever (or foolhardy!). Lose 30 points.

R Can one ever have enough housekeeping money? Are you a friend of Mr. Montague's? Check clue 5 and lose 25 points.

S The fact that he almost missed the train was of less significance than his physique, but neither has too much bearing. Lose 25 points.

T Smoking can be fatal! Award yourself 150 points and read the Truth, p.60.

58

A He wasn't suspicious but certainly suspecting. Lose 25 points.

B If you know who's who, you're a good detective! Award yourself 200 points and read the Truth, p.60.

C You're half right, but Miller's not the right person. Read the statements again and lose 25 points.

D She looks innocent. Try again and lose 20 points.

E Sharpen your powers of observation and your judgement of character! Lose 20 points.

F Doesn't accord with the evidence. Lose 25 points.

G You can sometimes judge people by their appearance and in this case it helps. See clue 40 and lose 10 points.

H You're going to have to sharpen your powers of detection; you're too easily convinced. Check clue 46 and lose 25 points.

I Asking the maid not to look in seems reasonable. Your answer doesn't; lose 25 points.

J You missed the most important clue. Check clue 59 and lose 20 points.

K Right on both counts, but wrong about him. Check clue 42 and lose 20 points.

L Appearances do count; opportunity is not always enough. Award yourself 100 points and read the Truth, p.62.

M So you think he did it! Well you haven't taken notice of all the evidence. See clue 13 and lose 30 points.

N Dead men don't bruise. Lose 25 points.

O People who are about to commit suicide don't endorse cheques. Lose 25 points.

P Just because his boots were muddy does not necessarily connect him to the crime and if he has a good alibi, can he really be the one? Check clue 19 or 29 and lose 25 points.

Q Use logic! Lose 25 points.

R Are you suggesting the lovely lady engineered the theft of the pearls for the insurance money? Only a cad would. Lose 25 points.

S You haven't proved your case at all. Try drawing yourself a plan. Lose 30

points.

T You've missed important evidence. Check clue 4 and lose 10 points.

67

A You're letting prejudice influence you. Lose 25 points.

B You've got to sharpen your wits, and your eyesight. Lose 20 points.

C If he didn't have a strong motive, he's not the kind to kill for pleasure. Lose 25 points.

D You'll have to prove both your assumptions; but I doubt you'll be able to. Lose 30 points.

E Everything was arranged to suit him — even his interpretation of Jensen! Award yourself 150 points and read the Truth, p.60.

F Not much point then to his attack. Lose 25 points.

G Is this plain prejudice or do you have some evidence? See clue 40 and lose 10 points.

H Half right. Check clue 31 and see if you can solve it. Lose 25 points.

I There are too many curious incidents for a simple case of suicide. Check clue 3 and lose 25 points.

J You're right. His overspending got him into trouble. Award yourself 100 points and read the Truth, p.60.

K Are you suggesting he was in "cahoots" with someone? He wasn't! Lose 30 points.

L You show an obvious unfamiliarity with opportunity and character. Lose 20 points.

M You're right on both counts, but then he's no suspect, is he? Lose 20 points.

N Suicides don't normally wear glasses. Lose 25 points.

O You've missed an important clue. Check clue 55 and lose 25 points.

P If the boots have no bearing on the case, why would you think Black would doubt his alibi? Perhaps it's you who are prejudiced? Lose 25 points.

Q His behaviour was perfectly consistent. It's your thinking that's wrong.

Lose 25 points.

R Are you suggesting her husband was penny-wise and pound foolish? Lose 25 points.

S Athletic prowess is not the vital clue to this crime, though it helped. See clue 12 and lose 20 points.

T You've got me confused as well as yourself. Lose 10 points.

68

A Suspicious, no, except about Hoxton's luck. Lose 20 points.

B You've missed important evidence. Check clue 36 and lose 10 points.

C Then he's obviously not the man. Try again and lose 30 points.

D Have you found other evidence against her? If not, lose 25 points.

E You don't give him enough credit. Check clue 15 or 25 and lose 10 points.

F Doesn't seem much of a suspect. Maybe he didn't really exist! Lose 20 points.

G So why else do you suspect him? See clue 52 or 40 and lose 20 points.

H Too many mistakes can be murder. Award yourself 150 points and read the Truth, p.62.

I Seems obvious there's more to this case than a simple suicide. Check clue 3 and lose 20 points.

J No marks for detecting here. Lose 10 points.

K Your answer shows an unfamiliarity with routine. Lose 25 points.

L He was certainly best placed to gain entry at all times. Try again and lose 10 points.

M Not much of a suspect — no motive, even if his alibi isn't good (which it is). See clue 13 and lose 25 points.

N Dead men don't bruise and suicides don't wear glasses! Lose 30 points.

O Your powers of observation need sharpening. Check the story again, or a couple of clues, 55 and 62. Lose 30 points.

P Inspector Black was too good a detective to conclude that muddy boots and a reasonable alibi

would tell against Sykes. Lose 20 points.

Q That seems to let him out. Lose 20 points and try again.

R Aha! You think the Montagues were trying to keep up with the Joneses. Not very charitable, lose 25 points.

S You've guessed right about Purcell — nothing about him is significant — but wrong about the culprit. Lose 25 points.

T You've missed vital evidence. Check clue 4 and lose 20 points.

911

A Neither is true. Lose 30 points.

C You're half-right. Study the pictures carefully and try again. Lose 10 points.

D Right on both counts. Award yourself 75 points. If you can find his accomplice, you'll get extra points.

G Would a brother steal from his sister — especially when he had plenty of money? Lose 25 points.

I Are you certain there's specific evidence? Lose 30 points.

K He'd only have talked about it if it were a conspiracy. It didn't appear to be; lose 25 points.

L Both "clues" indicate he was murdered. Lose 25 points.

M You think this man needs to be watched but not from my evidence. See clue 23 and lose 30 points.

N He's a nasty piece of goods. Award yourself 50 points if you haven't realised he had help. Read the Truth, p.61.

O Are you suggesting he tried to pin it on someone else? He didn't; lose 25 points.

Q Part of your answer doesn't agree with the evidence. Lose 10 points.

R You've made him out a very devious character, which isn't at all correct. Lose 30 points.

S Even if he knew about the gems, he wasn't in any position to put his hands on them. Clue 12 will show you why. Lose 30 points.

T You'll need real evidence to back up your suspicions. Lose 25 points.

912

A Neither has much bearing in the case. Lose 25 points.

C You're seeing something where nothing is, and nothing where there's something. Try again and lose 20 points.

D These answers show you haven't considered the crime carefully enough. Try again and lose 10 points.

G You're obviously not conversant with trust funds. Lose 30 points.

I Your answers conflict. Check clue 61 and lose 25 points.

K So how can you account for the fact that he did mention it? Lose 20 points.

L You've missed an important clue here; lose 30 points.

M His spirit was willing, but his flesh was weak. See clue 13 and lose 25 points.

N The evidence points to murder not suicide. See clue 8 and lose 10 points and guess again.

O You're wrong on both counts. There's plenty of evidence against another — lose 30 points.

Q You're right that the evidence points to her. Award yourself 150 points and read the Truth, p.61.

R Money is the root of all evil — but he wasn't that evil. Lose 25 points.

S Well, if he didn't know, why suspect him? Lose 25 points.

T These answers cancel each other out. Lose 30 points.

1011

A You're half right, but no further along in solving the case. Lose 25 points.

C You're right. The Inspector's case rested entirely on a slip of the tongue. Award yourself 100 points and read the Truth, p.60.

D The evidence is before you, but you haven't reached the correct conclusion. Lose 10 points.

G So why would you suspect him? Lose 20 points.

I Do you think she's covering up for somebody? Not so. Lose 25 points.

K Your reasoning is incorrect. Lose 30 points.

L Clean hands and a teacup point to murder, not suicide. Check clue 67 and lose 20 points.

M No motive, no proof, no suspect. Lose 25 points.

N Are you being reasonable by suggesting he wasn't? Lose 10 points.

O You're right, but it obviously wasn't him who did it. Lose 20 points.

Q You've missed vital evidence. Check clue 17 and lose 20 points.

R A nasty character it seems, only it's not so. Lose 25 points.

S Even if he knew, he was in no position to take them. Lose 25 points.

T Motive isn't enough in this case. Check clue 33 and lose 20 points.

1012

A While both answers are correct, he's the wrong suspect. Lose 20 points.

C You can't recognise a good clue when it's placed right before you. Lose 10 points.

D You think he did it all on his own, but he couldn't have. Lose 20 points.

G Doesn't seem much of a suspect. Check clue 10. Lose 25 points.

I Not a very good suspect, then. Lose 20 points.

K You can't be certain of the latter but definitely of the former. Lose 25 points.

L A good detective must interpret the evidence cor-

rectly. You haven't. Check clue 67 and lose 25 points.

M Doesn't seem much of a suspect. Read the story, look at the pictures carefully and try again. Don't forget to lose 20 points!

N The evidence doesn't agree with you. See clue 56 and lose 20 points.

O You've underestimated his powers of observation and overestimated your own. Lose 25 points.

Q You don't have a solid case yet. Check clue 17 and lose 10 points.

R Seems to be in the clear. Check clue 32 or 45 and try another suspect. Lose 20 points.

S Two "no's" don't make him right! Lose 20 points.

T Not much of a suspect. Lose 25 points and try again.

1315

K Neither was the case. Lose 30 points

Q If he knew the proper envelope wouldn't he have made a better job of things? Lose 25 points

R You're letting your prejudices get the better of you. Lose 30 points.

S Right on both counts, but now you know he didn't do it. Lose 20 points.

1316

K Would he have just hoarded the gem, then? Lose 25 points.

Q Right answers, wrong suspect. Check clue 27 and lose 20 points.

R Nothing to go on except prejudice. Lose 25 points.

S You missed a vital clue. See clue 22 and lose 25 points.

1415

K Such a singular stone could never have been sold surreptitiously. Lose 25 points.

Q Not even warm. Check clue 27 and lose 30 points.

R Does he need to cover his tracks? The evidence points elsewhere, so check clue 32 and lose 25 points.

S I don't think you have a clue as to how it was done. Read the story again, and lose 25 points.

1416

K There's no real evidence against him. Check clue 42 and lose 20 points.

Q You've missed something. Check the story and try again. Lose 25 points.

R Seems innocent enough, which he is. Check clue 32, 45 or 5 and lose 20 points.

S Wrong on both counts. Clue 22 should be helpful here. Lose 30 points.

1719

K Right both times! Award yourself 200 points and read the Truth, p.60.

R This line of thinking won't get you anywhere: lose 25 points.

1720

K You've missed vital evidence. Check clue 35 and lose 10 points.

R Why do you think he's the culprit? Lose 20 points.

1819

K You've missed vital evidence. Check clue 2 and lose 10 points.

R Too bad. Both red herrings. Want to see a real clue? Check clue 32 and lose 30 points.

1820

K Then why do you suspect him? Lose 20 points.

R Two red herrings, but I would have thought the séance a better guess. Lose 25 points.

THE TRUTH

D Solving this case was mere child's play. Of course the kidnapper had had inside help. Someone had stepped on the tube of lotion lying in the spilled powder, but it wasn't the kidnapper. He left muddy footprints, with no trace of powder. Someone inside must have stepped in the powder and cleaned their own prints after the kidnapper left, either leaving his on purpose, or not noticing them because the mud had not dried. Miss Woodcock may have told the truth, but the secretary was definitely lying. At 1:13 a.m. the light in the baby's room, still on in the morning, must have been shining. If Miss Dapple was sitting up in bed in the dark she must have seen the light showing beneath the door, since her bed faces the door to the nursery (see pic. 2).

B This was no accident. There were no signs that the girl had slipped and stunned herself in the bath. The way her hand clenched the sponge proved that she had been conscious when she went under the water. The maid told me about the girl's headache and the aspirin. She had lifted the glass off the carafe, put it on the table, then stirred in the aspirin. There should have been two sets of fingerprints instead of one. Henrietta wanted the £200,000 left to Isabel. She killed Isabel by raising her legs while she was in the bath, thus drowning her. She wiped the tumbler clean then impressed Isabel's fingers on it, which would have proved that she, Isabel, had taken the aspirin. But she impressed them only once. Henrietta exchanged rings, watches and handbags with Isabel, and called out "Henrietta" when she saw her. But she forgot that Isabel's hair was not permed (note her straight hair in the bath). What was a "perm" receipt doing in the supposed "Henrietta's" handbag?

A Hoxton had been seated when he was stabbed. Somehow, he had dragged himself across the room to pick a flower from the vase before he died. "Why would a dying man bother to do this?" I asked myself. He must have wanted to leave a message behind. There was no pencil among the contents of his pockets. (He'd had to borrow one, as you may recall, to tot up his winnings.) Hoxton had been trying to reveal the identity of his murderer! I quickly realized that I needn't cross-examine Price or Seymour, but Bloom certainly deserved my full attention.

K I guessed from the direction of the blow to Quackenbush's body that the culprit was a left-handed man. I had each suspect sign a statement, and observed that only Vincent was left-handed. (You may have noticed this in pic. 5, which shows him spreading butter on his bread.) I also found a medal among the coins beside Quackenbush's body. He must have grabbed this from Vincent's watch-chain as he fell.

J Here is where my skill in observing details was called to the fore. I noticed there was a change in pictures over the fireplace (see pics. 8 and 10). The bullet passed through Mrs. Davenport's head at an upward angle, and lodged in the picture frame, cracking the glass. If she'd shot herself before falling across the bed, the bullet would have gone into the wall behind the bed, not above the fireplace, which is on the opposite side of the room. Davenport's changing the pictures when I left the room was sufficient ground for suspicion. The hairpins on the carpet near the fireplace might have fallen during a heated argument.

T It's funny how bad habits run in families. William's small flat must have been murky when the brothers met that evening, for all three of them were smoking. Even old Throckmorton enjoyed his cigarettes. However, Tom is the only pipe smoker, and it is his smoker's companion lying on the floor among cigarettes. Tom certainly won't get his promotion now — but he will be spending plenty of time indoors.

C Miss Peattie may have been a great actress, but she wouldn't have won an award for forethought. When I held up the gun in a handkerchief, I hadn't told the actors that Marks had been clubbed and not shot. The natural reaction to a gun as a murder weapon is that the victim has been shot. Therefore, Miss Peattie's remark gave her away immediately. The metal piece from Miller's costume probably fell off earlier in the evening, and was placed on the desk for safekeeping.

E I've heard plenty of cock'n'bull stories from suspects, so I didn't take Sandhurst's statement too seriously. For one, if he had left his servant drunk and in bed, why wasn't the pillow dented? And even if Jensen had got up again to swill more bottles, how did he open them? Sandhurst cunningly arranged empty bottles and corks around the room, but forgot to leave a corkscrew.

Was I supposed to believe the soap "set-up?" Freak accidents do happen, but if Jensen had slipped, the soap would probably have shot clear across the room!

P

Percy Carrington was the vile murderer. What gave me the first clue was Halliday's walking stick. It wasn't his at all — at least, not the one found near the body. Halliday must have leaned heavily on his stick while waiting for his rival, for there were circular impressions in the ground around the tree, and also one on the envelope. But the ferrule of the stick I picked up was much too small to have made impressions like that. If you have a keen sense of sight, you would have noticed Halliday's bandaged leg — he must have been using a stick with a rubber tip for safety reasons.

But Carrington's stick was perfectly clean from the tip upwards for a space of about two inches; the end of the stick had been protected. The fellow obviously grabbed the wrong stick in his haste and later, seeing his mistake, threw the rubber tip away.

If you thought that the bit of dirt on Sykes' boots was real evidence against him, your name is mud!

N

Mrs. Hamilton and her brother-in-law were passionate people, but certainly not murderers by nature. They acted on impulse, leaving a scene covered with clues. First of all, if Mrs. Hamilton had killed the rope herself, the knife would have only frayed the rope until the last few strands snapped. The rope couldn't have broken so evenly (see pics. 1 and 3). Secondly, a dead body cannot bruise. Hamilton got that bruise before he died. Finally, his dusty suit, the scratches on the heels of his shoes, and the dust in tracks near the door showed what really happened. Hamilton had been stunned — or perhaps killed — by a blow on the head, dragged along the floor on his back, and hanged in the attic. The clean-cut rope revealed that someone had held up the body when the rope was cut. Neither Mrs. Hamilton nor her brother-in-law could have carried out this gruesome task alone. That meant they were in it together.

S

This thief obviously had so much on his mind, he forgot to wear his gloves. His fingerprints gave him away. I found the telling prints on the off-side door of Mr. Poswaite's compartment. Poswaite, however, was not sitting on that side, but on the near side. The door handle that Poswaite turned to board the train was on the right-hand side of the door, away from the engine. Therefore, the door on the off-side must have had its handle facing towards the engine. If someone had inched along the footboard toward Poswaite's compartment from the front of the train, he might have grabbed hold of the window with his left hand, but to do so with his right hand as well would mean moving past the door and opening it backward onto himself. This is a highly unlikely occurrence. However, if the thief came from the rear of the coach, he would necessarily pass the door to reach the handle, probably holding onto the window frame as he did so. There were two men in compartments behind Poswaite's, and one, Scofield, was wearing a fingerstall. Dalston, then, was my man.

F

Tavistock put his foot in it that time! His statement was an out-and-out lie. There were footprints leading *away* from the house (see pic. 5), but none leading *towards* the house — obviously an inside job. Also, Miss Danbery thought it strange that the letter was addressed to Superintendent Peters, but wasn't it stranger that the letter she brought out was addressed simply to "Superintendent of Police"? (Note different stamps, too, pics. 10 and 12.) Someone had switched the letters. That's probably why her belongings had been scattered when I first found her; they'd obviously been searched. The first letter must have identified the forger. Who else but Tavistock would have known that the letter Miss Danbery carried was so important? He killed Danbery, then attacked the daughter from behind as the only way of retrieving the letter. He must have substituted the new letter while she lay unconscious on the settee and I was investigating outside. (Afterwards, I did find the burnt ashes of the original letter beside a candle in Tavistock's room.)

M

As old Mortimer Snatchet says, "Time is money." And the thief in this burglary case would certainly agree. As you may have observed, and this case depended entirely on visual clues, Jasper needed one hour to get to work — he left at 8:30 each morning to arrive at 9:30. A journey there and back would have taken him two hours, so he couldn't have stolen the money between 11:00 p.m. and 12.20 a.m. Pearl also took nearly an hour to reach the office. Since it would have taken him almost two hours for the double journey, I would rule him out too. Garnet, however, got to work in half an hour. He could have made a trip to the office and back in an hour, with about 20 minutes to carry out the crime. And don't you think there is something odd about a candle that was the same length at 12.20 as it was at 11:00?

Q

It has been said that the director's secretary knows more than the director. In this case, the secretary knew too much — namely, the combination to the safe. Because Greyson's room and safe were entered so easily, I knew that the thief had to be someone who was familiar with his office. But whoever stole the plans had been uncertain as to which envelope to open.

Greyson, Jarrold and Fiske all knew which was the correct envelope. That left Miss Young. Also, the envelopes had been cut with a pair of scissors having small curved blades, which left curved cuts along the edges of the paper (pic. 10). It only took a moment to find the nail scissors in Miss Young's bag (which you saw her using the previous day, pic. 3) and then a few minutes more to elicit a full confession from Miss Young.

O It wasn't difficult to suspect foul play in this so-called "suicide" case. Firstly, it was August 11th, and a warm night (the partners and clerk were in their shirts-sleeves), yet the electric fire in Knight's room was burning. Also, why would a man about to commit suicide bother to endorse a cheque?

The little shreds I picked up from behind Knight's desk meant nothing to me until Reeves said that he had thought it strange to see a toy balloon on Deay's desk before he went out to post a letter (see pic. 2). When Reeves ran into Knight's office upon hearing the report, he noticed some shreds near the gun on the floor. Here is my theory: Deay shot Knight while Reeves was out posting the letter. The junior partner had picked an opportune moment to get the clerk out of the office, since the letter could have been posted the next day, there being no collection that late at night. Then he blew up the balloon and turned on the fire. When he heard Reeves return, Deay tied the balloon to the heater and went into Reeves' room with some papers. The heat of the electric fire burst the balloon, creating the sound of a revolver going off. (The revolver was of .22 calibre and would have accounted for the muffled sound.) While Reeves phoned the police, Deay dashed in and removed the balloon end and string from the fire, but missed the pieces in his haste. He also forgot to turn off the fire. I did find the other shreds of balloon in Deay's room.

L You might say that I caught the man red-handed in this case, although the actual colour was black. I immediately suspicious of the sour old landlord when I spotted his ink-stained hand. The suicide note on Simmonds' desk had been written with a pen dipped deep into an ink bottle, thus the long inky mark on the paper. But the dead man's hands were spotless — he couldn't have held that pen before he died. Peck's hands were clean, too. The conniving Quigley must have planted Peck's handkerchief in the hope of framing him.

G Solving this crime was not, for me, a long drawn-out affair. As you may have noticed, the chair in the hall had been moved to a point just beneath where the Colnaghi had been hanging (pics. 2 and 7). It had been used to reach the picture. Neither Hodgson nor Waverly would have needed a chair, as you can tell by a comparison of heights. Steinmetz, however, was a noticeably short man. He would have needed the chair to reach the picture. Moreover, when he put his foot on the chair, the side of his shoe had caught the back. Ordinarily, this would only have caused a graze, but Steinmetz wore spats (pic. 5). Spats have buckles at the side. The sharp buckle of Steinmetz's spat made a deep scratch, which P.C. Hobbs noted. Had the young constable asked Mrs. Carruthers for a detailed description of each of her visitors, he would have had no trouble in solving the case. (The ransacked bureau was probably set up to suggest a common burglar.)

R Mrs. Montague had powdered her back and shoulders before going down to dinner (note her powder puff, pic. 3) and the thief, in grabbing the pearls, brushed her shoulder with his sleeve. A good detective would have seen the powder mark on Crabtree's sleeve (pic. 1). Disposing of the pearls was another matter. When I arrived, he had to conceal the pearls and trust to luck to getting them back later. The wine decanter on the table seemed the quickest possible solution. While I was examining the table, Crabtree must have slipped the pearls into the decanter under pretence of helping himself to a cigar. (Did you notice the altered levels of the decanter and the fact that the cigar box had moved?) Only one man was smoking a cigar, so I had no hesitation in arresting Crabtree.

H Poor Mr. Bickerstaff may have been destitute, but he didn't take his own life. In order for him to have melted the sealing wax used to seal up the door he would have needed matches. Although I did find some used matches on the floor near the door, they were safety matches. This type of match must be struck against a box in order to light, but there was no box in the room. While safety matches can be struck against glass or some other surface, they always leave marks, and I could find no marks or scratches anywhere. Bickerstaff, then, could not have sealed the door. Someone else must have knocked him out, sealed the door, turned on the gas, and escaped through the window, which he left slightly open in his haste.

I If only some of our detective sergeants were as perceptive as Dr. Crumbom! After receiving a phone call from young Coombes, I went straight to the station and asked the good doctor some very specific questions about the Cavendish home. When he made his evening visit to Mrs. Cavendish, there had been two knitting needles in the wool on her table. The next morning, there was only one. He found part of a broken needle on the floor. He saw the other part of it, with string round it, first in a drawer in the study, and later peeping out of Mr. Cavendish's pocket (see pics. 3 and 11). Cavendish must have been in his wife's room the night she died. Dr. Crumbom suspected him of pouring laudanum into the linctus, which would have disguised the taste. The key to the locked door mystery lies in the broken knitting needle and the piece of string. My sketch of how this apparatus works helped Crumbom and Coombes understand how Cavendish carried out his devious crime. The device works very well on a well-oiled door. After the key has been turned, the needle falls out and can be pulled through to the other side as long as the door has a good clearance underneath.

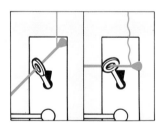

ACKNOWLEDGMENTS

Dorling Kindersley Ltd. was helped in this production by many people and companies, most specifically by Scotland Yard's amateur dramatic society, The Comets, under the direction of Brian Whitehall. Our special thanks go to James Munday, a member of the troupe, who played Inspector Black. We are also grateful for the assistance of The Lambeth Players under the direction of Bernard Dandridge. To all those who either acted, lent space or props, or contributed to the design, we would like to extend our thanks.

THE CAST

The Comets Dramatic Society
Paul Adams, Stewart Barrett, Kim Beeton, Roger Berry, Steve Bethell, Herbert Cable, David Coward, Phyllis Davey, Jill Docwra, Yvonne Docwra, Alan Faulkner, Yvonne Green, Debbie Grisely, Dave Halliday, Terry Harris, Dave Hughes, Alan Johnson, Richard Mellor, Mark Milkowski, James Munday, Jim Nicholson, Maureen O'Brien, Frank Penton, Eric Peterson, Derek Pitts, Peter Pugh, Geoffrey Reeves, Maureen Roddy, Barbara Scales, Bill Sharp, Peter Smith, Graham Spencer, Tony Tobin, Paul Toscani, Brian Whitehall, and Bob Wilson.

The Lambeth Players
John Alexander, Bernard Dandridge, Bruce Douglas, Betty Grzybek, Elisabeth Lowe, Richard Luxford, Joanna Newth, Jason Prichard, Jill Prichard, David Potter, Eileen Ryan, Lesley Scott, Robert Silver, Mike Stevens, Roger Stotesbury, and Dennis Vaughan.

Other actors
Chris Baldwin, Denise Brown, Sophie Carroll, Derek Coombes, Steve Cutts, Steve Fawcett, Fred Houlan, Mike Houlan, Stuart Jackman, Dolly James, David Lamb, Ian Marr, Bernard Martin, Fred May, Melanie Miller, Terrence Monaighan, John Patten, Steve Purvis, Simon Redington, Annabel Riggs, Dominic Sagar, Brian Shelly, Phil Wilkinson, and Evelyne Yan.

PHOTOGRAPHY

Jan Baldwin
Concerning Colnaghi, 10–11
Death of a Lodger, 14–15
Dead Man's Tale, 18–19
Industrial Espionage, 20–21
Going for Broke, 22–23
The Basil Street Incident, 24–25
An End to Life, 26–27
Accidents Do Happen, 28–29
Theft at a Seance, 30–31
The Kidnapped Baby, 32–33
Motive for Murder, 34–35
Diamonds Aren't Forever, 42–43
Colour shots on pages 2, 3, 11, 17

Paul Fletcher
Final Curtain, 6 9
A Rendezvous with Death, 12–13
Bridal Grief, 16–17
The Purloined Pounds, 36–37
Locked Room Mystery, 38–39
Robbery on the Paddington Express, 40–41
Black on the Beat, 44–45
The Park Lane Affair, 46–49
Colour shots on pages 7, 10, 14–15, 20–21, 24–25, 29, 32

Locations
A special thanks to The Basil Street Hotel; The London Transport Museum, Covent Garden; and The Park Lane Hotel, Piccadilly. We are also grateful to the YWCA Central Club for permission to photograph in their Lutyens building.

Props
The carpet used in "Accidents Do Happen" was from a selection at Barkers of Kensington.
Thanks to Mysteries, London's Psychic Shop, 9 Monmouth Street, WC2 and to Mark Dunn, Phyllis Gorlick King, Peter Scally and James Scally from Covent Garden Antique Market.
The Lost Weekend, Peckham, was helpful in locating period clothes.

Design
Debra Lee

Illustrators
Kuo Kang Chen
Kathy Wyatt

Photographic Services
Derek Robinson Partnership
Les Greenyer

Typesetting
Alan Sutton Publishing Ltd., Gloucester

Reproduction
Repro Llovet, Barcelona

Master Record of Police Cadet

Cases investigated	Points earned
Final Curtain	
Concerning Colnaghi	
A Rendezvous with Death	
Death of a Lodger	
Bridal Grief	
Dead Man's Tale	
Industrial Espionage	
Going for Broke	
The Basil Street Incident	
An End to Life	
Accidents Do Happen	
Theft at a Seance	
The Kidnapped Baby	
Motive for Murder	
The Purloined Pounds	
Locked Room Mystery	
Robbery on the Paddington Express	
Diamonds Aren't Forever	
Black on the Beat	
The Park Lane Affair	

Total score

Great uncle Henry's marking system became the basis for promotions throughout Scotland Yard. Compare your score with these ratings to locate your rank within the force. Should you have earned more than 3500 points, do not hesitate, but go directly to Scotland Yard and demand an office.

Scotland Yard Ratings:

0–500	Police Constable
500–1000	Sergeant
1000–1500	Inspector
1500–2000	Chief Inspector
2000–2500	Superintendent
2500–3000	Chief Superintendent
3000–3500	Commissioner